C. S. LOVETT

DEATH: GRADUATION TO GLORY

Some years ago my father-in-law went to be with Jesus. I was kneeling beside his bed just hours before his departure. He couldn't speak. Cancer made his jaw immovable. But he could faintly squeeze my hand and blink his eyes. I asked him if he was looking forward to seeing Jesus. His eyes lit up and his hand trembled. I sensed he was trying to tell me something. The Holy Spirit led me to ask,

"Hal, are you trying to tell me you are anxious to get out of this body and on to the great things Jesus has for you?"

With his remaining strength, he squeezed my hand vigorously. I found myself actually shaking hands with him. It took me a moment to realize the Spirit of God was prompting me to congratulate a man who was about to "graduate."

Shortly he was gone. All that was left was a dead body, one full of disease. What should we do with it? Hal was through with it. So was the Holy Spirit. None of us wanted it for anything. Since the arrangement had been taken care of in advance, I made the one phone call. The body was taken away and we never saw it again. That was a blessing, believe me.

• A few days later we had the service here at our PC chapel. It was NOT a funeral service, neither was it a memorial. It was a *"graduation"* service. After all, Hal had done the greatest thing a man can do — receive Christ as his Savior. Thus his future was far more exciting than his past had ever been. So instead of looking back, which funerals do, we honored him for being in Christ and what that meant to his future. Christians should be regarded as "graduates." For that is exactly what they are.

Let the world weep and cry. Let it cling to its pleasures, its bodies and also all it counts as precious. Our God has granted us things that even our imaginations will not fully hold. Therefore we must not behave as those who feel the end of man is dust. Christians can meet death with a shout. **A shout that shocks.** And the world is shocked when it sees God's people marching through death's door beaming like children. No one can die like a Christian. When Christ sets us free, it is from the rudiments of this world. We are no longer bound by the traditions of men. And the insights of this book can let you say to the fearful,

"There's nothing to it."

DEATH: GRADUATION TO GLORY

by

C. S. LOVETT

M.A., B.D., D.D
Director, Personal Christianity

Author of
Dealing With The Devil
Soul-Winning Made Easy
"Help Lord—The Devil Wants Me Fat!"
Jesus Wants You Well

**Illustrated by Marjorie Lovett
and Linda Lovett**

Published by

**PERSONAL CHRISTIANITY
BOX 549
BALDWIN PARK, CALIFORNIA**
1978 edition

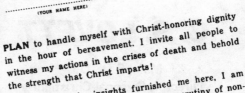

BE IT KNOWN THAT, I

....
(YOUR NAME HERE)

PLAN to handle myself with Christ-honoring dignity
in the hour of bereavement. I invite all people to
witness my actions in the crises of death and behold
the strength that Christ imparts!

BECAUSE of the insights furnished me here, I am
confident my behavior will pass the scrutiny of non-
christians and present a startling witness to the resurrection and the life to come!

IN THE GRACE OF OUR LORD!

PRINTED IN THE UNITED STATES OF AMERICA
by
EL CAMINO PRESS
LA VERNE, CA 91750

CONTENTS

INTRODUCTION

"SCAREDY CAT, SCAREDY CAT..."

When I was a boy, our gang used to swim the irrigation ditches that laced the San Joaquin Valley. One day we came upon a wide canal with the water running very swiftly. Should we try crossing it? At first it seemed we were all too afraid. But finally one lad was brave enough.

We held our breath as he plunged into the swirling current. Anything could happen. And though the water carried him some way down stream, he made it to the other side. He climbed out and stood proudly on the opposite bank and shouted to us:

"Come on. There's nothing to it! See, I'm OK!"
That was all we needed. Someone to go ahead and

show us how simple it was.

"Come on. There's nothing to it! See, I'm OK!"

And so it is with death. Mankind is held in awe by it. People have stared at it and wondered . . . and speculated . . . but Jesus has already plunged through it to the opposite side. And He too stands there calling:

"FEAR NOT, I have overcome it. I am He that liveth, and was dead: behold I am alive forever more!"

Isn't that fabulous! The Lord went through the experience of physical death that He might announce to us ... it's perfectly harmless! The mystery has been removed. We see death for what it really is — the greatest adventure of human experience. Can you appreciate how fabulous that is? Death is nothing more than an exit from this life into the next. When it is time for us to leave the earthly school of sorrow and suffering, we graduate into the presence of the Lord. Hey! That's what death is for the Christian — **Graduation to Glory!**

C.S. Lovett

Chapter One

INSIDE LOOKING OUT

John Quincy Adams was 80 years old when a friend asked:

"Well, how is John Quincy Adams today?"

"Thank you for asking," he replied, **"John Quincy Adams is quite well. But the house in which he is living is becoming rather dilapidated. In fact it will soon be quite unlivable and I shall have to move out any day now. But John Quincy Adams is quite well, thank you."**

This American Statesman had allowed a great truth to find its way into his daily life. He had learned that John Quincy Adams was an ageless being who lived inside a body subject to the decay of time.

THE LESSON OF THE COFFIN

 Funerals are good for something. They teach Christians a truth easily learned from the Bible, but one which registers better when demonstrated. The next time you attend a funeral where the body is displayed, stand for a moment before the casket and look down, let the obvious move in you as never before:

MAN IS NOT A BODY — HE HAS A BODY

The man is gone but his **complete** body is there. What can this mean? Man is not a body — he merely has a body. Oh yes, it's true. Look at the corpse again. It's all there, isn't it? Brain and all.

Ever have the thought go through you, that while every body is equipped with a brain, **someone has to use it?** When a brain operates by instinct alone, the result is a beast. A brain is a tool for thinking man. **A person uses the brain.**

It is hard for us to picture a person apart from his body. But that is because we seldom think of him any other way. We have to think of practically everything in physical terms. But before you have finished this chapter, you will begin to think of people as completely separate from their bodies.

But you were looking at a corpse. And you did notice that the **man was gone,** didn't you? Of course. And he didn't take his brain with him, did he? He didn't need it, that's why. For he also has a **mind** — a mind which belongs to his person as his brain belonged to his body. Now don't gasp, that's not the

10

real point anyway. Probably you're asking, **"Well, if he left the body behind, what kind of a "form" does he have now?"** Good. Your thinking is right on target. But will it be all right to answer that a bit later?

PSYCHOLOGY OFFERS THE SAME LESSON

Find it disturbing to learn that someone lives inside your body? That it is merely a tent or temporary dwelling? One day it will become unusuable either through age or damage and the person inside will be forced to evacuate! Well, if you are meeting this truth for the first time, don't be overly exercised about it. Psychology has been probing it for 100 years.

Psychology is the study of the man who lives inside the human body. And those who work at this rather new science know very well that he is an **unseen** individual who gets his information about  the outside world through the five senses. And apart from what he can gain by means of these, he is in total darkness. It's true. Take the eyes for example. They are devices which scan and distinguish between patches of light and dark and send them to the brain, via the nerves, as impulses. There they are interpreted into images. Thus, human eyes are like a periscope for the person inside. Put out those eyes and he has no visual contact with the outside world.

And so it is with the ears, hands and other senses. They too, send information to the brain and the man inside uses it to interpret the data. So modern space telemetric systems are not so new after all. Man has been analyzing metered data since the beginning. But notice, without these sensory detectors, man could not get along well in this world. In fact, were his senses to be totally destroyed, it would be the **worst form of solitary confinement.** But at the same time, this unveils the human form for what it is — a kind of **space craft** for the beings inside.

 Psychologists are excited when they discover something new about the concealed being. They have developed clever schemes and devices for getting him to project himself — permitting the clinicians to learn more about him. Tests like Rohrshach, Thematic Apperception, Sentence Completion, etc., provide clues enabling investigators to construct a personality profile. Amazing, isn't it? Almost any psychologist will tell you there is a sort of "fun" that goes with playing detective with the scraps of evidence that combine to expose the **personality** inside the body.

THE MAN INSIDE

If one is not a body, what is he? We are not merely offering the obvious when we say **he is a person.** Until one becomes familiar with the distinction between **person** and **body,** the statement remains quite profound. A person is composed of three non-physical elements which combine to give him his personality. And these are the **intellect,** the **emotion** and the **will.** It is the operation of these **unseen** features which make us what we are — people.

If anyone wishes to argue that intellect, emotion and will can be seen, ask them for a bucket of love or a pound of wisdom. But be laughing when you do and they will see the point. You do not mean, of

12

course, the expression of these things, but the intrinsic, spiritual elements of personality themselves. Thus, they will agree that man is essentially a spirit-being. And maybe go so far as to agree that part of him at least is unseen. They will go further than that later on.

Now the Bible speaks clearly on this; man is made in the image of God.* It is true that his body is formed out of the dust, as is any other physical thing, but the rest of him is of the **"breath of God!"**[†] **In the day of his creation he stood up on the earth the most unique thing under the sun — the image of God inside a two-legged vehicle,** hidden from every eye except God's. Who'd suspect a "replica" of the Almighty was housed within this earth bound creature! Think of it. God's own image walking about in an **earth-suit!**

The New Testament affirms, **"No man hath seen God at any time,"**[‡] but the very same thing can be said of the image of God. **"No man hath seen the image of God at any time,"** either. This means that no one can see you. They can see your body, that's true, and even become accustomed to your behavior pattern. They think they know you. At least they can identify your words, actions and expressions. **But no one has ever seen you.**

Now take identical twins, really identical twins. They are not identified by their looks, but by their personalities. It is just the outward vehicles that are identical, the persons inside are different. Thus, one exhibits a mode of behavior different from the other, and the cute little expressions and reactions of one will be quite different from the other.

---

* Gen. 1:26   † Gen. 2:7   ‡ 1 John 4:12

Does it seem frustrating to be hidden from view, to think that we know people when really we don't? Actually, we don't even know ourselves. Not now, anyway, but one day we will. In the unveiling, **"then shall I know, even as I am also known"*** says Paul. Look in a mirror, what do you see? A pair of eyes and that familiar face. You smile, but behind those good looking features resides a person you have never seen. You think you know what he is like, but you don't. All that you can see is that ingenious "earth-suit" housing the image of God.

The reason you are wearing the "earth-suit" is because **you belong to another world.** You are a spirit-being and your natural habitat is the spirit-world. And for you to appear on earth you need an "earth-suit." Since this is true of the image of God it is also true of the Object. God, Himself the original Spirit-Being,† must also put on an earth-suit to **appear.** And He did. Our Lord Jesus is God in an earth-suit! And unless He put one on, there would be no way for Him to reveal Himself as a man.

When Jesus said, **"He that hath seen me hath seen the Father,"** did He mean that men were finally able to examine a spirit-being? No, not at all. He meant that the person reflected through His words and deeds, was God. That the Person they beheld manifested through His body and behavior pattern was the Almighty Father.‡ In Jesus Christ we have the full **reflection** of the Person of God, but the **essential being** of God remained veiled, even as we.¶

---

* 1 Cor. 13:12   † John 4:24   ‡ John 14:9   ¶ Heb. 10:20

14

YOU ARE IN JAIL

Did you know your body is a prison? It is. The earth-suit, while it gets you about on this planet, is actually a **prison of the soul.** Take the image of God and limit him to merely natural functions and at once he is in jail. Did you know also, that as the image of God, you have capacities far greater than your body can possibly serve? Given a body that could keep pace with your capabilities you could make Superman look like a 90 pound weakling. So, even though you are the image of the omnipotent, omniscient, omnipresent God, you are **temporarily restricted** to this earthly container. As long as you remain in a physical body there is very little you can do. You can only go as fast as two legs can carry you, work as your arms have strength and all your thinking is limited to the brain that comes with your body. Designed for the eternities of heaven and your soul capable of spanning the ages, you can only know the things that come to you through the five senses. The image of God is forced to **putter with finitude** as long as he is stuck in a body.

INCOMMUNICADO!

 You are being held **incommunicado.** A spirit-being, who will one day fellowship with the spirits of men, you may not do it until released from the prison. **No contact is allowed.** You are not even permitted to see the God who made you. You must remain in darkness as far as the spirit-world is concerned. You hear nothing spiritual, see nothing spiritual and feel nothing spiritual. None of us likes being cut off from our natural habitat, but it is only for the time of our earthly sojourn.

At once you ask, why? The answer is obvious, though we cannot take time to deal with it fully here. Consistent with the **faith principle,** we are **"momentarily"** cut off from the realm of our true existence, i.e., God's immediate presence, and restricted to earth.* In accordance with His plan to give men free choice, God has found it best to remove them, for a time, from the splendid glories of the spirit-world (heaven). In His wisdom, He has chosen to reveal Himself in Jesus Christ, as a man on the earth, rather than to have us know Him amidst the splendor of His majesty and omnipotence. In this way, men can behold the **graces of His Person** and not be blinded by the glories of His wealth and power. And it is only as men receive Christ can they ever hope to see God.†

THE FRAIL JAIL

Your body is a living thing. Its life is **completely separate** from the man inside and it belongs to the animal kingdom. It was formed from the dust as were all the other animals. And were you not using it, or better, were not God using it as an earth-suit for His images, it would have its place with the other creatures. Then, of course, it would be controlled by **instinct only.** But now it is subject to you and yours to do with as you please. The one you have may be pretty or otherwise; it may be healthy or not, it may be tall or short, whole or crippled, but it is yours and is exactly the one God ordered for you.

What a masterpiece of design and ingenuity! Doctors marvel when they behold the fabulous planning of the earth-suit. And David praised God as he found himself "fearfully and wonderfully made."‡ It is

---

* Phil. 3:20
† For a fuller treatment of the faith method see, "The Thrill of Faith."
‡ Psa. 139:14

so beautifully conceived that before sin wrought its full destructiveness, the human body could last for centuries. Adam remained in his for more than 900 years and Methusala broke that record. It is written that when our Lord returns, creation will be restored and men's earth-suits will once more endure for centuries.*

CREATION OF ADAM
What a masterpiece of design and ingenuity!

---

* Isa. 65:20

 But now science is doing its best to hold the line at age 59. At least insurance tables are based on this figure. And this is somewhat below the three score and ten we have been led to expect. Actually, the prison of the soul is **quite frail.** As marvelous as it is, it barely holds us. Fail to feed it and it quits. Fail to clothe it and it will freeze. Expose it to disease and it can be fatally corrupted. Hit it too hard and it can be fatally damaged. It seems a shame to hurry the process, but men do. They put guns to their heads, jump off bridges, and take chances on the freeways. But one doesn't have to wait too long. Age itself can make the organs cease. So, as marvelous as it is, the earth-suit is quite delicate and requires care if it is to endure any time at all.

BUT ONCE YOU ARE OUT!

If you are disappointed when you see your photograph, don't feel too bad. You won't look that way long. And if you're tempted to fret over your I.Q., forget it. Intelligence has to do with **brain equipment only,** and that is a part of the body. You are a lot smarter than you presently suspect. And if you resent being stuck in a two-legged animal which hopelessly fails to match the flights of your imagination, just wait. It will all be changed.*

Talk about space ships, why they will appear ridiculous compared to the way you will mobile in the spirit. You will travel at the speed of **thought!** And that reduces the speed of light to a sluggish crawl. Wonder how long it took the Apostle Paul to make it

---

* Phil. 3:21

18

to the Third Heaven? Probably the **twinkling of an eye.*** But that is only one surprise, there are others. A moment ago we said you could only go as fast as your body could take you and your thinking was limited to the brain that came with your body. Maybe now you can guess what awaits?

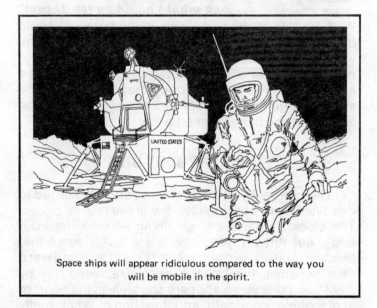

Space ships will appear ridiculous compared to the way you will be mobile in the spirit.

Remember when Jesus was tempted in the wilderness? And how that Satan was able to show Him all the kingdoms of the world in a **"moment of time?"**† That's the way things are done in the spirit world. Jesus was instantly exposed to the glories of all nations. Boy, that's the way to cover territory. It awaits, so don't get too disturbed if arthritis slows you down. It is just for a time.

---

* 2 Cor. 12:2
† Luke 4:5

In my congregation is a lady 85 years old. She is severely crippled by arthritis, but still manages to hobble around and serve the Lord. She complains occasionally, **"Oh, if I only had a nice young body like you folks, look what I could do for Jesus!"** Well, it's true. If she had a nice young body she could do many things she cannot now. But actually the woman is not old. She is ageless and I get a kick out of reminding her of it. Her body is 85, but she is just a kid at heart. Put her in a body that could do it and she would jump a six foot fence. Her body may be aging, but she hasn't gained a day.

ONLY THE BODY DIES

The moment you were born, your body started to die. With every passing day, the grave moved closer. The clock may tick off remaining seconds for your body, **but not for you.** There is a lovely verse that teaches quite the opposite: "Though our **outward** man perishes, the **inward** man is renewed day by day,"* and this verse appears squarely in the heart of a discourse on death and the body. What really happens is that we mature through experiences, but we do not age. Our persons acquire experience and undergo gradual change as we are moulded into the image of Jesus. But you will be the **same age at death as you were at birth** — just wiser. So the grand old hymn is true, "When we've been there ten thousand years . . . " we will not have aged a bit.

Don't you enjoy handling such treasures of truth as these? Suppose you could somehow be

---

* 2 Cor. 4:16

transplanted from your present body into a younger one, and when that body aged, transplanted again. Why, you could remain on earth indefinitely. Though I can't think of any reason why a Christian would want to, unless of course, he has not yet sampled the insights of heaven. But God will not allow such a thing, for He has **"appointed unto men once to die, but after this the judgment. . . ."*** Let science work as it will, here is one transplant it won't make. They can't even find a man, let alone stuff him into another carcass.

Our Lord featured this truth in still another way. Hear the Master Teacher speak of death again, **". . . Except a corn of wheat fall into the ground and die, it abideth alone: but if it die, it bringeth forth much fruit."**† Those who plant can appreciate this most.

One watermelon seed can produce a whole vine full of melons each packed with seeds.

---

* Heb. 9:27   † John 12:24

One watermelon seed for example can produce a whole vine full of melons and each of those packed with seeds. And it is true our Lord was speaking of His death in just this way. He was eager to get on to the great work of building His church and this lay after His physical death. But look again at the figure He used. This is what interests us.

A seed must go into the ground and there allow the outer shell to decompose and release the inner life. The one who can fathom the mystery of life within a seed can appreciate the scheme of God which places us, His image, in these bodies. Without the death of the body there can be no release. And while our dear Savior was referring to His release to a larger ministry, the seed illustration is a giant clue. **The outer shell must give way, before the man inside can be released.**

A kernel of corn must go into the ground and decompose to allow the plant to bring forth more ears full of kernels.

There is another intriguing reference by our Lord to this very thing. It passes almost unnoticed in Luke's Gospel. "I have a baptism to be baptized with: and how am I straitened (restricted, imprisoned, constrained) until it be accomplished."* The great G. Campbell Morgan has a significant paraphrase of this:

> "There are things I cannot do today. I am straitened. I have come to cast fire. My supreme passion is the fire should be cast. But it cannot be cast until I have been baptized with my passion baptism; and until it is accomplished I am restricted."†

Today men are clowning when they talk of being in a "strait". And another slang way to put it is to say that one is in a "bind" or a "fix." But none of these can do justice to great, heart-bursting, feelings that swept over His Majesty. Men were taunting Him when this cry escaped His lips. But see it as another clue!

Inside that body was the Almighty God! Men were provoking the Holy One, but may I say reverently . . . **in a straitjacket!** Yes, and I mean it most humbly, when I say Jesus Christ is God in a straitjacket! And those bonds were about to be shattered by the death process. Think of the awful compression! The Prince of Heaven restricted to natural functions so that He sat at a well and asked a woman for a drink; and again, "I am hungry, have you anything to eat?"

What a moment death was for Him. The release from His body was like escaping a tomb — the real tomb. It must have been a strange mixture of feeling. In some ways He eagerly looked forward to it. He wanted to get out of the body and get on to the building of His church. But in other ways He dreaded

---

* Luke 12:50
† The Gospel of Luke, G. Campbell Morgan, Revell 1931. P. 159

it. We see that in His constant sorrow as He faced the cross. What fantastic humiliation this! The mighty God no longer a spectator to humanity, but its central figure. And when death finally arrived, it ushered Him into the work He wanted to do for men. For Pentecost, with its miraculous fanfare, can only be our Savior . . . released from His prison to begin His supernatural work in hearts!*

What a moment death was for Jesus. The release from His body was like escaping a tomb.

So why shouldn't we be intrigued with death? If it permitted our Lord to have His fuller ministry in the Spirit, why not us? If it allowed Him to step out of His prison and into the freedom of the spirit world, why not us? He has already demonstrated its harmlessness and revealed it to be only a **stepping stone to greater things.** So it is natural to explore it

---

* John 14:20

for the joy the Holy Spirit has for us. Our next chapter turns the microscope of faith on high power as we examine our own escape from the straitjacket of this life!

Chapter Two

"JAIL BREAK"

A little mound marked the resting place of a small body. The headstone had but three words:

"Johnny!" As if someone had called.

"Yes, Father!" As if someone had answered.

Isn't that precious? A child answering the call of his Heavenly Father. And likely the family took comfort in this classic verse — most of us do:

"For WE KNOW that if our earthly house of this tabernacle were dissolved, we have a building from God, not made with hands, eternal in the heavens." *

---

* 2 Cor. 5:1

"JOHNNY!"
"YES,
FATHER!"

But wait a minute. There is something puzzling about that verse. Paul says, "We know." Could the Apostle be a bit too generous here? DO we know? And do you suppose Johnny's family really knew he had slipped out of his earth-suit to discover heaven's glory and his real self that same instant?

We are pretty sure that Paul was aware of such things — his letters give considerable space to them. It seems easy for him to shift from earthly to heavenly things, and we expect it of Paul. But I wonder if he can mean it when he says, "we know?" I doubt if very many evangelicals can say "we know."

WE KNOW WHAT?

"For we know that if the tent which is our earthly home is destroyed (dissolved), we have a building from God, a house not made with hands, eternal in the heavens."

Observe carefully the tense of that verb, "HAVE." It does not say that we hope to have, or expect to have, but that we **already** have a building from God. We have it right now. Scholars might say the "if" demands a "then" to give a future tense. But I submit that we have **RIGHT NOW** a building from God. Does that seem incredible to you?

You are aware of course, that should anything happen to you this instant, you are equipped to live in the presence of Jesus **forever.** That is, should death strike your physical body suddenly, you will not be found naked, but clothed with your "house from heaven." There's a deeper significance, **you have your eternal form this moment.** It's unseen, of

27

course. That's the meaning of the words, "not made with hands."

Did you know that? Paul seems to think we all should. But please be careful with my words. **I did not say we have the resurrection body.** I said only that we have the **eternal form** or building in which we will live in the presence of God — and there is a big difference. The resurrection body is for the resurrection. The eternal body is for heaven. These are two separate concepts, two separate experiences.

The eternal form, often referred to as the "morphe," the Greek word for **form,** is related to the spirit-world. It is a part of the spirit-world, therefore unseen. And it is this form which we have in the presence of God, Who is Himself a Spirit.* The resurrection body is a **physical** one and we will have it at a future time for our reappearing on earth. When Christ appears, we will appear with Him and for that appearance we will need a special body.† It will be our resurrection body. More on that later.

OUR UNSEEN HOUSE

If we are absent from the body and immediately present with the Lord, what kind of a **form** do we have? We will not use the word body, now, to avoid confusing it with the resurrection body. Whatever this "building from God" or form, it is as suited to the spirit-world as our physical bodies are suited to the physical world. In it, we will be able to see God as He is. And we will be just like Him.‡ We shall also be able to see each other as we really are.¶

Now let's take a look at the verse which precedes our text, yet is in the same context:

---

* John 4:24   † Col. 3:4   ‡ 1 John 3:2   ¶ 1 Cor. 13:12

"For the things which are seen are temporal; but the things which are not seen are eternal."*

If the FORM or "building" we have from God is "eternal in the heavens," then it is **unseen.** If it is unseen, then it is **spirit.** If it is spirit, there is nothing to keep us from having it right now. It is one of the splendid by-products of receiving Christ, **"Who has blessed us with every spiritual blessing in heavenly places. ..."†** Are we out of order to consider the spirit form as one of the spiritual blessings we have received in Christ? Hardly.

Now someone says, "Are you saying that a man can live without a physical body of some kind?" Indeed I am. And more than that, I am suggesting that **a person lives continually** whether he is in it or out of it. And later you will find me saying that he can shift from one to the other and scarcely be aware of the change. The change, which is called death, is just that simple and harmless. Doesn't the doctrine of immortality demand that man's life be entirely separate from his body? Is that not what immortality means, that whether a body lives or dies, it has nothing to do with the man himself? He is eternal. The life of the soul and the life of the body must therefore be **two separate lives.**

Now hear of the Apostle Paul's experience:

"I knew a man in Christ above fourteen years ago (whether in the body I cannot tell or whether out of the body I cannot tell: God knows) such an one was caught up to the third heaven. And I knew such a man (whether in the body or out of the body, I

---

* 2 Cor 4:18   † Eph. 1:3

**cannot tell: God Knoweth:) how that he was
caught up into paradise, and heard un-
speakable words, which it is not lawful for a
man to utter."** *

Please observe that the body played no part in the
transition from flesh to spirit. It made no difference
to Paul's **person** however it was accomplished. The
person had no regard for the body. You see the
Word of God does not admit to such a thing as the
soul being dependent upon the body for existence.
Contrariwise, **a man has his own life directly from
God.** And that life, like God's, is eternal. It is this
feature of man that makes the proclaiming of the
Gospel so urgent. All men are going to **exist
somewhere** — either with the Lord in heaven, or
separated from Him in hell — **regardless of any
body.**

But let Paul instruct us further as to the separa-
tion of the body; **"Knowing that whilst we are at
home in the body, we are absent from the Lord."** † It
is his clear teaching that anyone who would see the
Lord will have to get out of his physical body to do it.
And, in that moment of release, the Christian is
found clothed with a "form" that permits him to see
God as He is! So determined was Paul in this, that he
yearned to be absent from his physical body that he
might be present with the Lord. This is what he feels
when he says, **"To die is gain."** ‡

What is the "form" like? It will be like God Who is
Spirit. That's all I know. My brain will not hold or handle infinite concepts. My present apparatus cannot
conceive of being two places at the same time. Yet, I
am persuaded that we will be many places at one
time in the spirit-world. In fact, if we are to behold

---

* 2 Cor. 12:2-4   † 2 Cor. 5:6   ‡ Phil. 1:21

God, Who is **omnipresent,** how can we, except we be of the same order. That's big, isn't it? And if we are to be like HIM, WHO IS OMNISCIENT, we will have a lot of learning to do. He will be teaching us things we cannot now handle **while we are limited to a brain.**

 And then there is power. Our "form" will be such that we can work with power that surpasses anything man has yet dreamed. We know of the millions of pounds of thrust it takes to explore space. But what about the power it took to fling the universes into orbit and hold them there! Well, we can only guess about adventures in power — but they will be fabulous. And the FORM we will need to operate in that realm? I haven't the faintest idea what it is like, but I know I have it . . . now. God says so.

Death cannot rob us of anything if we already have our house from heaven. So that much is settled. Don't you find it intriguing that we are **wearing it this moment, even if we are not aware of it?** Since it is spirit, we have no way of detecting it. We cannot touch it, examine it or study it. We do not have the tools to examine spirit things. That which is flesh is flesh and that which is spirit is spirit. They are two different worlds. So, we take it by faith as we do all else God has already given us.

THE WALL OF AWARENESS

Did you ever ponder the verse, **"And has raised us up together and made us sit together in heavenly places in Christ Jesus"*** How do you suppose

---

* Eph. 2:6

that is done? It is easier to conceive now, isn't it? Of course. The spirit form which we now have allows us to be with Him in the Spirit even though we are not aware of it. **Wherever He is, that's where we are.** Some have been content to handle this verse as merely speaking of our standing or position in Christ, but that does not fully exhaust the matter. This truth can easily be literal, **in the spirit.**

The key to this is **awareness.** We have a great many things which go on around us and in many of them **we actually participate without being aware of them.** But since they are spirit, we have no equipment for examining them. Take for example, **"wrestling against principalities and powers."**[*] Consider the angels that are sent forth as ministering spirits to serve "them who shall be the heirs of salvation."[†] And have you heard Satan actually speak his cunning into your ear.[‡] No, you have **contacted** none of these things, yet you do not question their reality. You have the evidence, the results, **but you have not encountered their shape or form.**

And it is a strange thing to be cut off from the awareness of who you are and what you are really like. You have capacities for thinking you can't use right now. You're not even aware of them. You have

capacities for travel you can't use. You're tied to a body which can only be in one place at a time. And you have strengths of which you know nothing, for you are limited to the muscle power of your earth-suit. Just think. You

---

[*] Eph. 6:12   [†] Heb. 1:14   [‡] 1 Peter 5:8

have all this and can't use it — a "superman" and can't show off. Well, that's life . . . on earth, that is.

WALLS COME TUMBLING

Put a man in a dark prison under sentence that he should not come out until the walls were fallen and how glad he would be to see that concrete crumble. That is death, the crumbling of our prison walls. **The bondage starts to end with the approach of body failure.** No one feels sorry when deliverance draws nigh. No prisoner resents the joy of freedom. And Christians step out of their old prison rags to be clothed with the brilliance of God's glory!

Death is like waking up to a new morning.

It is like a new morning. The old life seems but a dream, and there's a new vigor and refreshment that

33

goes with it. That's what it's like to shed these bodies and find ourselves before the smiling and beckoning countenance of God. Those who feared death might be a terror, look back and grin. Why it was nothing more than stepping from a prison to a palace; passing from a sea of troubles to a haven of rest; out of shame and reproach into the glory of Jesus! What a wonderful morning!

We awake in His likeness! **Ah, so death is waking up.** It is the alarm clock of heaven. The wall of the flesh is down. No longer is that old brain the best we can think, those arms the extent of our strength and those legs the limit of our travel. Wow! How ingenious is our God! Just imagine putting His own image in animal bodies and cutting them off from the spirit world! That was clever, and then to find out afterwards that we were in the spirit **and didn't know it.** Heaven was our home all along and we didn't comprehend. But how could we? We were traveling the faith route.

We didn't know it, but we were much like the old sailors who were warned that they were but 4 inches from death. All that separated them from the briny deep was the wood of the hull. If that were to be split, the vessel would plunge to the bottom. But with us, we are only an inch, or even less. **It is the thin wall of flesh that separates us from heaven.** We are that close to the world to which we really belong. Let something happen to that wall and we instantly find ourselves in the spirit. Heaven is but a heart beat away.

BREAKTHROUGH!

Some people, you know, have registered

---

* Col. 3:3; Acts 17:28

glimpses of heaven even before the body released its hold. Doctors and chaplains see this phenomenon once in a while. It's true, even before the earth-suit quits entirely, some are privileged to react to what they see or sense of the other side, and those who stand by are able to observe. Christian literature holds many testimonies of saints who have uttered thrilling exclamations at the approach of heaven's glory!

"The celestial city," said Dr. Payson, "is fully in my view!"

"I breathe the air of heaven," said Thomas Scott.

"Christ-Angels-beautiful! Delightful!" The last words of Dr. Hope.

"I see things I cannot utter!" said the Rev. Mr. Holland.

"They praise Him! They praise Him! What Glory!" said Dr. Bateman.

"Can't you see? Can't you hear? What a sweet assembly!" cried Edmundo Auger.

 And likely you have heard of even more glorious expressions. As a Chaplain at Los Angeles County Hospital I heard them. Oh, there is Glory a heartbeat away. And these scenes come crashing through as the body let's go of its life. What a joy it is to have the flash of awareness break through to illuminate the soul even before death arrives. And if the body is still operative, the expressions can be registered.

The 23rd Psalm is true, **"Yea tho I walk through the valley of the Shadow of death . . . Thou art with**

me." Even when consciousness is fading, the presence of Jesus comes swarming through. And while not all Christians are in a condition to report what they see, enough of them do to let us know that God does not allow any Christian to linger in darkness. There is no darkness at death. **We don't die alone.** Our Master escorts us personally. How can there ever be a fear when the Lord says, "Take My hand, there's nothing to it!" **We can enjoy it!** We can behold each step of the Glory Road!

One night, when a friend and I were camping in the woods, I took the Coleman lantern to gather wood for the fire. The glow of the lantern cast a circle of light about me. But just then lightning flashed over a distant range and for a split second the whole country — hills — valley — cliffs — were exposed to instantaneous view. I saw it. My eyes snapped like the lens of a camera. It was there in detail. And so it is at death. As the body begins to relax its grip, we are aware of only things around us and then FLASH — for an instant — even before we have departed the flesh:

"I see Him! He's beautiful! What Glory!"

And don't think you will mind stepping out of that body to be with Jesus. You won't. Who cares for old rags when riches are being donned? Who thinks of the cold when summer arrives? And what eagle ever  went sorrowing after its shell when once it was born? While it was yet unborn that shell was the eaglet's world, the thin wall of that little globe its protection. But once it had broken out to become an eagle of the heavens, it will not desire to return and cuddle those flaky bits in the nest. Nor will you have the slightest thought for the shell that was once your earthly home.

WHAT'S IT LIKE THERE?

Journey to the tropics and behold the beauty of its foliage and brilliant fruits. Bask in the glory of the equatorial region and let your mind be filled with its pomp and grandeur. Then travel North to the land of the Eskimo. Sit down with one who has never been out of his area and try to give him some idea of the tropics. The only things he can work with to form his image will be the moss and stunted shrubs that grow little higher than his feet. How can a man who has to grub the soil for berries know of oranges, bananas and pineapples?

How can an Eskimo who sits in the shadows of icebergs and glaciers know of tropical fruits and lush foliage?

Can one who sits in the shadow of icebergs and glaciers consider the lush wealth of rain and sun? Hardly. And so it is with us. We have new sensations of life coming for which we do not have the tools to conceive or consider. Only a few things are certain and clear. We will see Jesus . . . as HE really is!

Still, who can describe it properly? Can the Apostle John as he writes his revelation? No, the best he could do was speak of streets of gold and gates of pearl. Have you ever felt sorry for him? You might, for everything he used will be worthless in heaven. But the old disciple was doing his best to get what he saw in language meaningful to us. Silver and gems we can understand, but spirit things we cannot.

His problem was no different from that of Brother Paul. And you recall how he dismissed the whole matter as being of things **"of which it is unlawful** (that would be natural law) **to speak."** But then Paul was not instructed to write as John was. That's the problem isn't it? That which is flesh is flesh. And the flesh can only comprehend things of the flesh. And that which is spirit, is spirit. These are two different worlds and **"n'er the twain shall meet."**

No, there will be no bodies. Not as we know them anyway. There will be a FORM. A passage referring to our Lord **before the incarnation** is a healthy clue, **"Who being in the F O R M of God and equal with God. . . ."** It will be entirely suited to heaven — but note that **it is not a suit.** We will not need suits of any kind. This is our natural **environment.** The diver who goes into the water needs a suit. The astronaut who circles outer space needs a suit, but those in

38

their natural habitat do not. Heaven is our natural environment. It is on earth that we need the strange, animal gear. Heaven is home for the image of God.

But of the resurrection, we know much more. God has revealed some startling things about that. You will have a body and it will be an amazing one. Wait until you see what you will be doing in that body — that's next.

Chapter Three

THE NEW TUXEDO

"I'd sure like to be here when the Lord comes!" Ever hear that? Sure you have. What they are really saying is, **"I hope I don't have to die."** Death is feared as an awful experience and it is thought a fantastic blessing to escape it. People feel if they could somehow remain alive unto the coming of the Lord, they could miss the dreaded thing. But here is the surprise. We all die — even the ones alive when Jesus comes!

CAN'T AVOID DEATH

"Wait a minute!" You say, **"What do you mean we will all die. Doesn't the Bible state that the living will be changed when Jesus comes?"** Yes, it does and that's the point. **Death is a change.** Dr.

Norman Vincent Peale calls it a change into a new form of existence. He declares it to be a transition and nothing more. And he calls anyone who doesn't believe this, an **unfulfilled Christian.*** If we are changed, we die, for that is all death really is. If we are all going to be changed, then no one escapes.

Do you remember Enoch? He died. Oh, I know it says, **"that he should not see death."**† He didn't **see** it. He did not see death strike his body. That is, he did not see death in the sense of having **to watch his body die.** He escaped that, for he was **changed in a moment.** God translated him. But he died nonetheless. He changed realms. He made the transition from the physical to the spirit, from earth to heaven. And it is in that sense we say no one avoids death.

When the Lord comes again, the living saints make a transition from one form of existence to another. And like Enoch, they will not have to **watch their bodies die.** Therefore, they will not **see** death either. It will happen too fast to see — in the twinkling of an eye. The only advantage in being here when the Lord comes would be to miss any unpleasantness that might be associated with the body change, unpleasantness such as a bullet or cancer. That kind of longing is very natural.

What timid creatures we really are. Here is a precious experience and we know so little about it, we fear it. It is **fear** of death that binds, not death itself. And this is too bad, for it is truly a unique adventure. If the fear can be removed, Christians can anticipate death with delight. Strange as it may seem to you now, if the fear could be removed, **you could enjoy death!** You would honestly get excited at its approach.

---

* Guideposts April 1963   † Heb. 11:15

Think of being changed into the likeness of Jesus. What could be so bad about that? Surely it is no worse than a worm emerging as a lovely butterfly and that is an exciting improvement. But alas, we are so enslaved to the status quo we dread change, even when it is for the better. So we cling to this miserable realm, we hang on to this life and the old body when a better one beckons.

Turn now to a familiar passage. Notice its bold intrigue:

> "Behold I show you a mystery; we shall not all sleep, but we **shall all be changed.** In a moment, in the twinkling of an eye ... "*

Mysteries are being announced here. They have been hidden in God until Paul. Now they are ours to enjoy. And it is **within the Word of God** that we must explore, for anything else can only be speculation. When it comes to speculation, your speculator works as good as mine.

What we are keeping in mind, is that **everyone** goes through the transfer experience. The verse said, "we shall **all** be changed," didn't it? This means that no one is going to stay in his earth-suit forever. And if everyone is going to be changed, nothing is lost if a person's body should die before the coming of the Lord.

TO BE PRESENT WITH THE LORD

"Absent from the body ..."† that bothers you

---

* 1 Cor. 15:51, 52a   † 2 Cor. 5:8

42

doesn't it? What is it like to be out of the body and be found clothed with the unseen, eternal form — nothing more? Does just the thought of it make you feel naked? Are you picturing yourself wandering around in the limitless, spirit-world without any clothes? Well then, think of yourself as a puff of smoke if you must. But the truth is, when we shed these old bodies we do become disembodied spirits and **we will be very happy to be that way.** In fact, it is a splendid freedom such as we have never enjoyed before.

Now some suppose we will be itching to get back into a body again. We will be in our natural state — our eternal state — our happiest state — "our house from heaven."* **We will be just like Jesus.** If you can picture what He is like this moment — as He comes into people's hearts in the Spirit — then you have a picture of what it is like to be **absent from the body.**

You see, a man and a body do not belong together. They have no business together, for one is spirit and the other flesh. And they would not be together at all were it not for the **faith program.** For the purpose of faith (our earthly probation), God  has seen fit to blend the two and we find men walking around on earth in bodies. But certainly there is no thought of any kind of a body being needed for our spiritual existence. Bodies and the like belong to earth. Physical things are entirely out of order in heaven. It is for this reason a creature of heaven must don an earth-suit to appear.

So don't get too attached to that old body. You

---

* 2 Cor. 5:2

will drop it as quickly as a child abandons worn out toys when you find yourself in the presence of Jesus. And you won't care what happens to that old carcass once you enjoy the fantastic liberty of your **spirit-house.** A body will be the furthest thing from your mind. Unless, of course, you have occasion to revisit the earth. And you will!

WHEN JESUS RETURNS

At the center of Christian doctrine is the sweet fact that Jesus is coming again. And when He does, He will be visible. Prophecy says, **"every eye shall behold Him."*** And that human eyes may see Him, He will again don a body. For a spirit-being to appear, he must put on something that reflects light. Natural eyes can detect only those things which reflect light. This is the only way anyone or anything can **appear.**

Jesus' second appearance will be in glory! Ah! but notice. When He comes to appear to the world, so will we! This is a very definite truth:

> **"When Christ Who is our life shall appear, then shall** *ye also appear with Him* **IN GLORY!"†**

For us to share in the glorious appearing of our Lord, we will need **another** body. The old one we discard to rot in the soil or be consumed in flame. So we will need a **second** body. But since our Lord is appearing in glory, He will appear in a **glorified body.** And even though we have a glamorous spirit-house, **which is just great for heaven,** we will need another body if we are to **appear with** Jesus. But it will have to be one of Glory.

---

* Rev. 1:7   † Col. 3:4

It wouldn't do, you see, to wear the old style restrictive garments that we now use, on that grand occasion. It is going to be a formal spectacle and we have to be properly dressed for it. And we will. God has prepared for an another earth-suit, a **glorified** body. One which will be worthy of a King's companion. One which will be suited to His Majesty's presence on earth.

What a day it will be! The King appears amidst a flash of Glory! Of a sudden, men stop in their tracks to peer into the sky. Their eyes fix on the blazing spectacle. A trumpet blast causes everything to halt. For there . . . in the heavens . . . is the Great God! But let Him tell it:

"And then shall appear the sign of the son of man in heaven, and then shall all the tribes of the earth mourn, for they shall see the son of man coming in the clouds of heaven with power and great glory. And He shall send His angels with a great sound of a trumpet and they shall gather His elect from the four winds, from one end of heaven to the other." *

There He is! Not the Carpenter-Son this time, but the Most High God, crowned with Glory and honor. The Majesty of the Universes using the canopy of heaven as His royal carriage. And look who is with Him! We are! Here is the wonder. He

---

* Matt. 24:29-31

shares His triumphant return with us. What a fabulous honor. But that was the promise . . . **"then shall ye also appear with Him in glory!"** Talk about ceremonies, here is **"that blessed hope and glorious appearing of the Great God and Our Savior Jesus Christ!"***

This is our Beloved Lord in His returning glory. And we will be like Him. How will He look? Or, for that matter, how will we look? Like Him, of course, but only three people really know — Peter, James, and John. **They had a preview of this day.** Maybe it was so it would be written into the Record that these brethren were allowed to see our Lord **transfigured** on the mount:

> **"And He was transfigured before them: and His face did shine as the sun, and His raiment was white as the light. . . ."** (Matt. 17:2)

And later this same John wrote:

> **"His head and His hairs were white like wool, as white as snow; and His eyes were as a flame of fire; and His feet like unto fine brass and His countenance was as the sun shineth in his strength."** (Rev. 1:14, 16b)

The transfiguration of Jesus is a strange event. It stands out in sharp contrast to all else that took place in His earthly life, with the possible exception of the ascension. I can think of no more important reason for it, than to furnish a clue to the nature of things in the day of His coronation. I am convinced we have healthy insight here as to how He will look in the day of His reappearing.

_____

* Titus 2:13

Should you read the scene again, you will notice that it was a time for **reappearing,** for Moses and Elijah were there. And for them to be there they had to reappear. Their bodies had died centuries before. And I think we are on good ground to suppose that the transfiguration glory of Jesus is the same that He will display when He comes again. **And it will be ours, too.**

> "Beloved, now are we the sons of God, and it doth not yet appear what we shall be: but we know that when He shall appear, we shall be like Him. . . ." (Ist John 3:2)

In the day of His coming, the glory of our Lord will fill the earth. And we will be like Him. That means we will be present also in a glorified body! It will be fun for us to learn what that body is like as we track down other clues in the New Testament.

Keep in mind then that we have discussed three kinds of existence: **Our earthly life,** wearing this present physical body; **our eternal life** in heaven adorned by the spirit-house and **our appearing** with Christ in a glorified body. Now this raises questions, of course. But most of them will be answered easily if we keep these three states separated; earthly house . . . spirit-house . . . glorified body.

TRADE IN THE OLD BODY

Did you ever have the thrill of buying a brand new car? Have you made that delightful trip to the dealer to trade in the old family auto and drive off in a brand new one? This is probably one of the greatest treats of the American way of life, wouldn't you say? But did you ever think you might be trading in your old body for a new one? And I mean trade, not discard.

Those who are alive when Jesus comes will trade in their old bodies as one would trade in an old car for a new one.

Now some are going to do this. Who? Those who are alive and still in their old bodies when Jesus comes. Here's the Word on it:

"For our citizenship is in heaven, from whence we look for the Saviour, the Lord Jesus Christ: who shall *change* (notice that?) our body of humiliation, that it may be fashioned like unto His glorious body" (Phil. 3:20, 21)

It is trade-in time, when Jesus comes. No burying or cremating for those people. The old body is not put off, it is **changed.** Now aren't you glad we have the transfiguration scene recorded in the New Testament? Such a thing as our exchange of bodies would be a baffler if we didn't have that account as a clue.

When the Lord returns we will be busy with our earthly tasks, and suddenly we will hear the trumpet blast...and blink...we will be in our new tuxedos!

In the day of our Lord's return we will be busy with earthly tasks, just like anyone else. And then we will hear the trumpet blast and be attracted to the scene in the sky . . . blink . . . wham . . . we will be in our new tuxedos! The change will have been made and we didn't feel a thing. No pain, no sensation of any kind . . . it was too fast to feel. Who can measure the twinkling of an eye?

And then look! We find ourselves joining the heavenly band. Oh, what a glorious thing! No funeral for those of us who are alive that day. There's no body to bury. The old one is changed, just like the Master's that day in the mount. We've been transfigured!

It will take a moment to adjust and we're curious. So we feel this new body. It's solid. There are arms and legs. We touch our faces. Yes, it's a regular body, but then we notice something missed in all the excitement. WE'RE IN THE AIR! What kind of a body is this that operates in the air? How is it that gravity no longer binds us to the surface? And how come all this mobility? We will get to that when we examine other clues to this new glorified body.

 But isn't it a pretty good trade? We were moving along in an old carcass that was not only earth bound but beginning to wear out. And now look what we have! Wouldn't it be nice if one could trade a worn out car that way? Imagine exchanging the old family clunker for a glorified, atom-powered limousine! Well, that's the way things are when you belong to the One who can turn water into wine!

Now it's clear.

You always wondered about Enoch, didn't you? He left no body behind. And now it has happened to you. You didn't see death either. Your body didn't die, you were changed. Ah, so that's how it's done. The day of our Lord's coming will answer the Enoch riddle.

JESUS — RESURRECTED, BUT NOT GLORIFIED

What is a resurrection? The New World Dictionary says, in Christian theology it means, "The rising of Jesus from the dead after His death and burial." We can accept that. But I wish it had gone on to explain that this was the great sign the world was to receive and by it, know that Jesus Christ was all that He claimed to be.

Do you know about the sign of the resurrection? You should. Our Lord had made a remarkable prediction **about His body:**

> **"Destroy this temple (body) and I will raise it again in three days"** (John 2:19)

Isn't that an amazing thing for a person to say. Put this body to death and I will restore it in three days time. Now his audience didn't understand His words, but He was giving them a sign by which they would know that He was the Son of God. Here is His specific statement:

> **". . . An evil and adulterous generation seeketh after a sign, but no sign shall be given to it, but the sign of the prophet Jonas: for as Jonas was three days and three nights in the whale's belly; so shall the son of man be three days and three nights in the heart of the earth"** (Matt. 12:39-40)

No one had ever done anything like this. Oh, there had been resurrections. Lazarus, for one. Jairus' daughter for another, as well as the son of the widow at Nain. But imagine a man forecasting his own death and resurrection. **"Destroy this body,"** He said, **"and I will raise it up again in three days."** And now will you notice that it is the SAME BODY. Oh yes, Jesus rose in exactly the same body in which He died. Otherwise He would **have lied** about the sign. That was the sign, you see. And it was the same, even to the print of nails. Nothing was missing. Thomas, the disciple, could testify to that.

But now you're puzzled again, I hear you asking, **"But how could He get into that locked upper room if He had the same body?"** That is what you're thinking, isn't it? And because of this and some other unusual appearances after the grave, you conclude it had to be a different body. Right? I don't blame you.

JESUS TURNING WATER INTO WINE

Was not our Lord the Master of the Universes, even though He walked the earth in a human body? Did He not rebuke a storm to still an entire sea? Did He not make five loaves and two fishes satisfy an army of thousands? **When** did He turn the water into wine? The elements obeyed His command **before** the cross as well as after. And as far as getting into the upper room, do you suppose it was any harder than **walking on water?**

It was the same body all right. Our Lord was fulfilling the sign. And the death, burial and resurrection were all part of the same sign. The whole event was a single prophecy come to pass. And it was also the heart of Paul's Gospel.

"For I delivered unto you first of all that which I also received, how that Christ died for our sins, according to the Scriptures; and that He was buried and that He rose again the third day according to the Scriptures..." (1 Cor. 15:3, 4)

This was the great proof. Men saw Him after the cross. That is the way God planned it. **They were to see Him and in the same body.** That was the sign. His resurrection was proof. His body was proof. In fact, it was a proof-body. And here is the proof to the world:

"And that He was seen of Cephas, then of the twelve: After that He was seen of above five hundred at once: of whom the greater part remain (alive) unto this present ... " (1 Cor. 15:5, 6)

But then you noticed that some had difficulty in recognizing Him didn't you? And especially Mary. Don't be too hard on her. Neither she nor any of the disciples ever expected to see Him alive again. Mary went to the garden looking for a dead body, not a living person.* And this unbelief blinded her to the reality of His resurrection. But it was the same with Thomas. He looked upon the Savior in unbelief and it wasn't until he examined the nail prints that his faith broke forth in the wonderous cry.

 Take yourself, for example. You have a relative who lives in the East. Yet accidentally you meet him on the West Coast still believing him to be in the East. You just wouldn't believe it could be he. You would be struck by the resemblance, perhaps. But you would probably approach him with a cautious, **"John, it can't be you, can it?"** Don't bother to protest. Unbelief does this to all of us.

It was Jesus' reappearance in the **same body** that put the seal upon all that He had said. When a prophet says He will die, be buried and rise on the third day — **and does it** — men had better believe Him. Such a thing can only be done by God. But as we notice this, let something very significant strike home to your heart: **Jesus' resurrection body was not a body of glory.** It was not a glorified body. It was the very same one He had before the cross. So do not confuse any talk of Jesus' resurrection body with the glorified body of the saints. It is to His **transfiguration** upon the mount that we turn for that clue. And we have already reveled in that precious sight!

When He comes again, we will see our Savior **in His Glory . . .** and we will be with Him.

———————

* John 20:15

54

THE FIRST RESURRECTION

Did you know that after the resurrection of Jesus, many saints returned to their old bodies? And in those old bodies appeared to their friends in the city of Jerusalem:

> "And the graves were opened and many bodies of the saints which slept arose, and came out of the graves after His resurrection and went into the holy city and appeared unto many" (Matt. 27:52-53).

Don't you find it interesting that . . . "many bodies . . . arose?" The people didn't rise. Those saints were NOT in the ground, any more than Lazarus was in the tomb. Like Lazarus, these people were RESTORED. Their resurrection was nothing more than a restoration. Like Lazarus, they too **died again.** Now if by some miracle, similar resurrections should occur, even today, they would also be no more than restorations. The people would simply be returning to the same earthly life. This is NOT what the Lord promises us. The FIRST resurrection is going to be entirely different:

> "Blessed and holy is he that has part in the first resurrection; on such the second death has no power, but they shall be priests of God and of Christ and shall reign with Him a thousand years" (Rev. 20:6).

This was hardly the case with Lazarus, or Jairus' daughter, or the widow's son at Nain. They all died again. The first resurrection has to do with reigning with Christ on earth. It occurs just prior to the Lord's return at the end of the church age. All believers will participate in it, **including Lazarus.** He was merely restored that exciting day at Bethany. He will appear again in the "first resurrection."

JESUS RESTORING JAIRUS' DAUGHTER FROM THE DEAD

Would you want your old body resurrected — to die again? It was different in the case of our Lord. He gave His Word that He would appear again in the SAME body. That was the "sign of Jonah," for an unbelieving world. And because He did exactly as He said He would, time is divided into BC and AD. Every time a person mentions the year, it testifies to the resurrection of Christ. Who else has said to the world, "Destroy this body and in three days I will raise it up again." Who of us has claimed, "I have power to lay down my life, I have power to take it up again?" No one other than Jesus could give the world such a sign. The world has had its one and only sign until Jesus returns.

• The first resurrection is the TRUE resurrection. This is the one you and I anticipate. And the body we receive in that resurrection will NOT be this same old body, but a brand new one — a **glorified** body. The saints of all ages will be there. We'll see faithful Abraham as well as the Apostle Paul and Martin Luther, for they are all coming with the Lord. In that day the world will behold **"the coming of the Lord Jesus Christ with ALL His saints"** (1 Thess. 3:13).

We will have redeemed bodies.

Did you know your present body is not yet redeemed? That's true. It belongs to the animal kingdom and no part of the physical creation has yet been redeemed. So far the Lord has redeemed ONLY the souls of men. He has still to remove the curse from the creation. Even today death and disease do their dirty work, the big bug preys on the little bug, the strong devour the weak. It will stay that way until the Savior returns to be glorified in His creation:

"For the creation was condemned to become worthless, not of its will (the creation has no choice), but because God willed it so. Yet there is this hope: that the creation itself will **ONE DAY** be set free from its slavery and decay, and share in the glorious freedom of the children of God. (Rom. 8:19-21).

So far only your SOUL has been redeemed. That's all. The redemption of your body is a future event. You still live in a sinful, fallen world and your body is PART OF the unredeemed creation. Should your body be raised from the ground, after you die, and the Lord has not yet returned, it would again become part of the fallen creation. The world is WAITING for the day when the **physical** redemption will occur. But it won't take place until the sons of God are revealed. And they won't be revealed until the revelation of Jesus Christ. The day He is revealed, we will also be revealed. On that day, the physical world itself will undergo a drastic transformation.

The world is waiting for the day when the physical redemption will occur. On that day, the physical world itself will undergo a drastic transformation.

"For even at this present time (years after the cross) the whole creation groans and suffers an agony similar to the pangs of childbirth. Not only does the creation agonize like this, but we ourselves, who have the FIRST FRUITS of the Spirit, we too groan within ourselves, eagerly WAITING for our manifestation as the sons of God, that is, THE REDEMPTION OF OUR BODIES" (Rom. 8:22, 23).

When we participate in the first resurrection we will be wearing redeemed bodies. They will be glorious. Ever see an acorn? Do you know what it produces when planted in the ground? A mighty oak tree. Our old body may be buried in the ground in one form, but in the resurrection it will emerge entirely different. Paul says that the new body is totally different from the old, even as the seed buried in the ground is different from the harvest it produces. Paul cites a list of differences in the resurrection chapter. Concerning the old body, he says:

"It is sown a perishable body . . .
it is raised imperishable,

It is sown in dishonor . . .
it is raised in glory,

It is sown in weakness . . .
it is raised in power,

It is sown a NATURAL body . . . it is raised a SPIRITUAL body. (I Cor. 15:42-44).

PAUL'S SEED ILLUSTRATION

Were you to quiz the Apostle on the relationship

of the old body to the glorified resurrection body, brace yourself for a sharp reply:

"Thou fool (that means blockhead) that which thou sowest is not quickened except it die. And that which thou sowest IS NOT the body which shall be, but bare grain. . . ." (I Cor. 15:36, 37).

I warned you he'd be harsh. He thinks anybody should know something as elementary as that. And isn't he right? You sow a seed in the ground, but something entirely different surfaces.

 Certainly every farmer knows that, as do most housewives. People who plant flower seeds, for example, would be very unhappy if all they got back was the same seed. A resurrected seed would be a huge disappointment. One may plant a miserable tulip bulb in the ground, but a gorgeous flower appears. So it is with the TRUE resurrection body. It would be awful if all we could expect to receive was the same old body. That would be disappointing.

Have you ever seen a dirty, twisted ranunculus bulb? Terrible looking isn't it? Yet when you plant one, the resulting flower is an exquisite cup of glory! Is there a connection between the two? Yes, but one is certainly NOT the other. The bulb is sown in "dishonor", but it is raised in "glory." The same is true of our bodies. The old body is related to the new body, but one is not the other. The old body must not only die, it must DECAY in order to provide for the new. Every seed which bears fruit, must first decay **totally.** Obviously the same seed is never seen again.

60

THE RESURRECTION PROCESS

A remarkable thing happened when Jesus gathered His disciples to take leave of them for the very last time:

"**And when He had spoken these things, while they beheld, He was taken up and a cloud received Him out of their sight**" (Acts 1:9).

That was the way the Lord departed from this world.

"**And while they looked steadfastly into heaven, as He went up, behold two men stood by them in white apparel which also said, 'Ye men of Galilee, why stand ye here gazing up into heaven; this same Jesus, which is taken up from you into heaven, shall so come in like manner as ye have seen Him go into heaven'** " (Acts 1:10, 11).

Those in white were angels declaring the Lord would return to earth precisely as He left — **in the clouds.** Even as He physically ascended out of sight, so will He physically descend in plain view when He returns. He won't be alone, but accompanied by His saints — all wearing glorified bodies.

Where do they get these bodies?

Can we assume that the Lord **miraculously produces** the glorified body from the very **same clay** which made up the old body? Why not? I know it sounds a little weird. To the carnal mind such a thing is ridiculous. But I am writing for people who love the Word of God and believe that Jesus is able to subdue "all things unto Himself" and make them conform to His will (Phil. 3:21b). I'm not insisting on this view, but it delights me to ask, "Is anything too hard for the Lord?" The ways of the Lord are often foolishness to the carnal mind. What we're discussing here is for the spiritual mind only.

Is it not a trifle for the Lord to raise bodies that perish at sea?

● All right, so some bodies do perish at sea to become food for fishes. I understand how the basic elements of a single body could finally be spread across generations of marine life. Even so, God says ... **"The sea gave up the dead which were in it"** (Rev. 20:13). What else is this to mean? Certainly not the **souls** of men. And again, many bodies have been reduced to ashes with the elements entering into trees and plants, so that they become spread across generations of the animal and vegetable kingdoms. Yet, for those who have thrilled to God's might in the Word, is this not a trifle for the Lord?

How then does He do it? If this is what happens

just how does the Lord produce the glorified body from the original body? I haven't the faintest idea. I don't even understand how a tiny watermelon seed can end up as a whole vine producing millions of seeds. I just know it does. A farmer lives with the miracle of life out of death and he doesn't understand it. All he knows is that the seed must die and decay in order for the harvest to appear. It would seem that if the Lord could manipulate the elements sufficiently to feed a multitude (7000 people) with five loaves and two fishes, He should have little trouble producing new bodies from scattered elements.

NOTE: While I feel this is a simple thing for the Lord to do, I don't mean to press my conclusions on any reader. If you think God does NOT do this, that Paul's seed illustration is symbolical only, I don't mind. I can hardly claim to have the last word in an area where I have already admitted ignorance. I do feel, though, it is important to preserve the connection between the old and the new forms, even to the point perhaps of certain recognizable features. I draw this from the fact that (1) the event is called a resurrection. This implies a decided connection between the old and the new. Another word would have probably been used if there were no connection. (2) Paul's seed illustration at least implies that the new form emerges in some way from the old. When the actual event occurs, we'll all be too excited to care who was right or wrong about this detail.

THE FASCINATING PART

"Then the sign of the Son of Man will appear in the sky; then shall all the tribes of earth weep, and they shall see the Son of Man

63

coming on the clouds of heaven with power and great glory" (Matt. 24:30).

When the Lord comes in glory, He will make His appearance IN THE SKY! He will appear on the "clouds of heaven." I take those clouds to mean **clouds of saints!** This I believe is the "sign of the Son of Man." We are ALL going to be with Him, so the crowd won't be small (Col. 3:4). Also it is clear the world is going to witness the event. Just how various parts of the globe will see Him and the saints simultaneously, I don't know. But men themselves are doing remarkable things in the sky now. This appearance of the Lord in glory is His second advent, the great hope of the church:

"Looking for that blessed hope and the glorious appearing of the Great God and our Saviour Jesus Christ" (Titus 2:13). **". . .at the coming of our Lord Jesus Christ with ALL His saints"** (I Thess. 3:13).

When the Master returns He will be observed first of all in the midst of His people. He will be surrounded by His saints. And He will make sure they are ALL with Him before He sets one foot on earth:

"And He will send forth His angels with a great trumpet and they shall gather His elect from the four winds (those in the spirit) from one end of heaven to the other" (Matt. 24:31).

It is the Lord's plan that all of the saints should meet together IN ONE PLACE so that the entire party can make the descent TOGETHER. When they reach the ground, people who haven't been on this earth for centuries will be walking around in youthful and vigorous bodies. They will be marvelous bodies, yet not too dissimilar from the ones they had before. Remember how Moses and Elijah were somehow (perhaps intuitively?) recognizable when they appeared with the Lord on the Mt. of Transfiguration (Matt. 17:3).

See how the faithful of all ages will be with Him. No one is left behind. The Lord is going to BRING them with Him. Note that word BRING in this next verse. It's very important:

"**For if we believe that Jesus died and rose again, even so them which also sleep in Jesus will God BRING with Him (hold on to that word bring). For this we say unto you by the Word of the Lord (that makes it rather unshakable), that we which are alive and remain unto the coming of the Lord shall not precede them which are asleep**" (I Thess. 4:14).

Sleep is a term Jesus used to refer to people who have died.

NOTE: Sleep is a term Jesus used to refer to people who have died. You recall when Lazarus' body was dead, the Lord refrained from calling Lazarus dead. With Lazarus' body laid out in the tomb, Jesus said, "He is sleeping." Obviously it referred to the condition of the body. From the earthly point of view, a buried body assumes the position of sleep. We can't see the soul. This is why we speak of laying people "to rest" when we bury them. The soul of man never sleeps. Modern psychological tests show that even at the deepest levels of unconsciousness, there is considerable mental activity. We now know that physical sleep relates only to the CONSCIOUS process, with the unconscious furiously busy continually. Some of it even splashes up as dreams.

IN THE SKY!

Here we note something about those COMING WITH the Lord. Their bodies vanished from the earth ages before. Yet, here they are APPEARING with Him. For that, they need bodies. No one can make an appearance without some kind of a body. Those on earth cannot see spirits. If they are unable to see those with the Lord, then it is NOT an appearance. They must be wearing bodies in order to appear. They do. They are found in their glorified bodies BEFORE they descend to earth with the Lord.

But then we read something very strange:

"For the Lord Himself shall descend with a shout, with the voice of the archangel, and with the trumpet of God; and the dead in Christ shall RISE first ... " (I Thess. 4:16).

Oops! Did you see the word RISE! What is this? Do people themselves RISE from the ground? Think carefully now. Can souls rise from the grave? Where are these Christians? They are absent from their bodies and present with the Lord. We have dealt with that thoroughly. They are WITH the Lord when He returns, for He BRINGS them with Him. See now why I wanted you to hang on to that word BRING? Christians arriving WITH the Lord cannot rise, they can only DESCEND.

The mystery of bodies unravels when we note WHERE the Lord produces or assembles the resurrection body. When we see that, we answer the riddle of rising. The Lord does this instantly — in the sky! I repeat: if people are going to APPEAR with Him, they must ALREADY be wearing the glorified body when the scene bursts forth in the heavens. Therefore the Lord will gather the physical elements or produce the new form **simultaneously** with His appearing. Possibly He will do it with a word such as He did in the beginning. . . . "Let there be light . . . and there was light!" That's fast!

The instant the Lord appears in the sky, His saints appear with Him.

Now we have an answer to the riddle. The instant the Lord appears in the sky, His saints APPEAR with Him (Col. 3:4). Then the descent begins. Those **souls** who are already with the Lord do not rise from the grave. If anything rises, it will be their bodies. Indeed their bodies do **join** them in the sky. Yet it happens so fast no one can see it. People will not see bodies rising from tombs, floating upward to meet their owners. No, it occurs instantly on the command of Christ. The entire appearance is sudden! Later on you'll read about the **appearance method** to see how sudden it is.

> **OBSERVATION:** Please note how the resurrection occurs at the coming of the Lord. Bodies are not needed with the Lord in heaven. It is only when He is returning to earth that both He and His saints need bodies. The Lord is descending in glory and His saints appear with Him to share in His glory. There is no need for a resurrection until it is time for the Lord to rule on earth with His saints. Therefore the events recorded in 1 Thess. take place as the Lord is returning. He is on His way DOWN to plant His feet upon the Mt. of Olives as per the prophecy of Zechariah (14:4).

IN THE GROUND?

 Can it be said that anyone actually goes into the grave? The person is long gone before his dead body is placed in the ground. One look at a corpse is enough to settle that. The man who once lived in the body is obviously — **gone!** When a Christian dies, his soul is **instantly** with the Lord. When an un-

saved man dies his soul is **instantly** someplace else — awaiting judgment. Since the Lord died and opened the way into the "holiest of all," we go at once into the presence of God as soon as death strikes our bodies. We stay with the Lord from that moment on. Never again are we separated from Him for any reason whatsoever.

NOTE: Please, let none who reads this explanation of the true resurrection feel I do not believe in a literal resurrection of the saints. I do. I seek to show only that the PROCESS of the true resurrection is different from that which occurs in an ordinary resurrection such as took place with Lazarus, the Lord and the other resurrections recorded in Scripture. I think my explanation shows I firmly hold to a literal resurrection of the body.

The Apostle Paul used the figure of a seed sown in the ground and compared it with the new form which appeared above ground.

• When the Apostle Paul used the figure of a seed sown in the ground, and compared it with the new form which appeared above ground, he did so only to show the **relationship** of the natural body to the glorified body. He was NOT explaining the **mechanics** of the resurrection. He is not teaching that bodies actually surface like a plant breaking through the soil. He is teaching that the body we wear for our appearing is **mysteriously related** to the one laid to rest in the ground, just as a flower is **mysteriously related** to the decomposed seed which gave it life.

PETER RESTORING DORCAS FROM THE DEAD

Now in an ordinary resurrection, the soul **returns** to the old body. There is a restoration to the former life. In the first resurrection, the soul remains with the Lord and the **body joins the soul.** That is a genuine difference. Not only is there a difference in direction, but there is a difference in the body. When a man is restored, he **returns** to his same old body. But when a Christian appears with the Lord, he arrives in a new body. Thus, in the **true resurrection,** if the body does actually rise (in a flash), it joins that man. The

70

man himself DOES NOT rise but remains in the company of Christ. The body comes to him, he doesn't go to his body. This difference is not artificial. For only by such a process can a saint be found wearing a body when he comes with the Lord.

There is confusion if one pictures the TRUE resurrection as **people** rising from a grave. A restoration occurs that way, but NOT the first resurrection. Paul clearly states the Christians are coming with the Lord. They cannot be emerging from the grave if they are descending with the Lord. Therefore the **process** of the true resurrection is different from that of an ordinary **restoration.**

But what about us?

The dead in Christ get their new bodies first. But they won't have them long before we get ours. Not even seconds, I don't think. For no sooner are we, who are alive and remain on the earth, attracted to the amazing spectacle occurring in the heavens, then — BOOM — we're suddenly **changed!** Didn't Paul say "we shall not all sleep, but we shall all be changed?" (1 Cor. 15:51). Indeed. And how fast did he say it would happen? "In the twinkling of an eye!" One minute we're staring at the wonder in the sky. The next thing we know, we're part of it! And we don't feel a thing.

"For our citizenship is in heaven, from which we anticipate the return of our Saviour, the Lord Jesus Christ, Who, when He comes, will TRANSFORM the body we are now wearing, so that it will conform to the body He will be wearing when He comes in glory" (Phil. 3:20, 21).

We who are alive and still on the earth at the

71

Lord's coming skip the death process. At least we do not go through the chore of saying goodbye to our bodies as we head for life in the spirit with Christ. Instead, these very bodies (with us in them) are **changed** instantly. We don't go through the **"absent from the body and present with the Lord"** step. We go directly to meet Jesus in the sky **via a changed body.**

We who are alive and still on the earth at the Lord's coming skip the death process. We go directly to meet Jesus in the sky via a changed body.

● We don't even feel it. There is nothing to feel. Recall how the apostle Paul went through the experience of being caught up to the "third heaven?" And what did he report? "Whether in the body or apart from the body, I do not know. God knows. . . ." (2 Cor. 12:3). One second we're on the ground — "Blink" — the next instant we're with the brethren in the sky! Raptured. This is the rapture, and it is necessary if we are to be a part of the descending band. The Lord wants us with Him when He touches down on the Mt. of Olives. From that moment on we will be with Him IN PERSON — forever! Paul puts it this way:

"Then we which are alive and remain shall be caught up together with them in the clouds to meet the Lord in the air; and so shall we ever be with the Lord" (I Thess. 4:17).

Shades of Superman! There we are in the sky! We have joined the descending host.

Shades of Superman! There we are in the sky! We have joined the descending host. Now we are with the Lord and all those saints who went to be with Him ahead of us. Together we make the descent before the eyes of the world. But how is this done? What kind of a body travels through the air like this? And look — no oxygen tanks! And did you notice the speed? Wow! Surely we moved faster than the speed of light when we joined the crowd. That is but a paltry 186,000 miles per second. I am sure the glorified body covers space much faster than that. But just how fast, takes us into the area of speculation.

NOTE: The views expressed here represent the way the author sees the facts concerning the rapture, resurrection and revelation. He recognizes the Scriptures are not rigid in this area, but can be handled a number of ways. It might be necessary in some cases for sincere brethren to rearrange the events to harmonize them with their own eschatological positions. The author will not be a bit unhappy about that. The main thrust of this book is to show the harmlessness of death and the Christian attitude toward it.

THE NEW TUXEDO

Here is the realm of speculation. But if we trust the Holy Spirit to guide, we'll be all right. Part of our Christian privilege is to allow our imaginations to become a divine sanctuary permitting the Spirit of God to impress us with precious things. Of course, we dare not insist what we say is final. That would be foolish. And what we discuss here must be open to any further light the Lord would supply.

 Have you ever submitted your mind to the Holy Spirit for illumination? When our thoughts are saturated with the Word of God and our experiences interpreted by the Holy Spirit, there is impressed upon us something of the invisible. Our miraculous God is able to stamp living things upon our hearts. How else did the Apostle Paul learn? It is God's pleasure to reveal things to His children:

"Eye hath not seen nor ear heard, neither have entered into the heart of man, the things which God has prepared for them that

74

love Him. *But God has revealed them unto us by His Spirit,* for the Spirit searches all things, yea the deep things of God" (I Cor. 2:10)

Can we have the boldness to consider the glorified body? Is it wrong for us to dwell on the things God has in store? It is on account of them that we are willing to let go of this life. These things can make us eager to forsake the world and live Christ?

The Apostle Paul opens a great deal to us in his resurrection chapter. He has been comparing the old body with the glorified one.

"It is sown in dishonor; it is raised in glory; it is sown in weakness; it is raised in power: it is sown a *natural* body; it is raised a *spiritual* body" . . . (I Cor. 15:43-44)

There's the key. In Paul's comparison of the two bodies he finally comes out with it. The old body is a **natural** one. We know about that, we spent almost a whole chapter considering our imprisonment within it. But what is this **spiritual** body? Paul thought we might miss the point here, so he repeats the idea:

"There is a *natural* body and there is a *spiritual* body" (I Cor. 15:44b)

Of all the comparisons the Apostle makes, I think this is the one least noticed by observers. We won't make that mistake. The original Greek provides even more interest. The body we now have is a natural or "psuchikos" body. The one we will have is a spiritual or "pneumatikos" body. And these two Greek words give us our biggest clue.

First, let's consider the spiritual body. Now this is **not a spirit-body,** it is a **spiritual** body. They are not

75

the same. There is no such thing as a spirit-body. That would be like a filled vacuum; a black white; a round square; or a silent noise. You see they are opposites. That which is spirit is spirit and that which is flesh is flesh. They can never be mixed. But a spiritual-body is a different matter. This is a body **subject to the man inside,** or subject to the spirit. And what an advantage there is in having a body that is subject to you.

Your spiritual-body can't get tired. The energy is supplied by spiritual power.

It can't get tired, so there is no sleep and no beds. It will not need food. The energy is supplied by spiritual power, rather than an external fuel from food. Neither will it have to travel from place to place. You will say to yourself, **"I want to be in Cairo,"** . . . and phhht . . . you are there! Make it Paris, Argentina or Jerusalem if you like. That is traveling, and at the speed of thought ! Now, I didn't say we couldn't walk. Of course we can, if we want to. We will have two good legs. But the glorified body, being subject to the spirit, will be able to do something the old body could never hope to do — APPEAR and DISAPPEAR!

"I want to be in Paris or Cairo..." and phhht...you are there!

NOW YOU SEE ME—NOW YOU DON'T

 Do you know about appearances? The Bible is full of them. Learn of them and there will be far less mystery to the glorified body. We are not used to the concept and the thought startles us. We are so accustomed to traveling from one place to get to another. The only way we can mail a letter is for our two legs to take us to the mail box. But that's the natural body for you. You are its slave and you can only move as fast as those legs will carry you. But there is another way, the **appearance** way.

When our Lord Jesus ministered in Old Testament times, He would **appear** as the Angel of the Lord. In Abraham's day, **"... The Lord appeared unto him in the plains of Mamre. ..."*** and there follows a stream of references too numerous to list. Even in the days of His ministry in the flesh, He used the privilege when it suited the divine purpose.† But usually He traveled as we do, even to the point of becoming weary beside a Samaritan well. I am glad He used the appearance method, however, for it makes our study more sure.

But the angels give us an even more significant clue. They put on bodies to appear also. Did they not appear unto Abraham and walk with him down to Sodom? Those were real bodies, for the men of Sodom lusted after them. And Jacob met the angels of God, too.‡ Did not two men in white appear at the tomb of our Lord and then again at His ascension? Indeed.

---

* Gen. 18:1, 2   † John 10:39 ASV.; John 6:21; 20:19   ‡ Gen. 32:1

Remember the surprise of old Zacharias, the father of John the Baptist? When he was busy in the temple, **"there appeared an angel of the Lord standing on the right side** of the altar..."* And surely you recall when Jesus was agonizing in the garden, **"there appeared an angel unto Him from heaven."**† Of course, you do. And if angels can make appearances, it is not idle to suppose the sons of God will do the same. We are higher in rank. The angels are **"ministering spirits sent forth to minister for them who shall be the heirs of salvation."**‡ And when we consider that we are scheduled to **appear with Him** in glory, the matter is settled.

HOW DOES IT WORK?

You are in a dark room standing near the light switch. There is stillness as you reach out your hand. ..."Click" ... and light floods the room. "Snap," and it is dark again. With the command of your finger, the light appears or disappears. It is an instant. Think now of that light as a spirit-being. Upon command he appears and with another command, he disappears.

That is what it is like to be a spirit-being and **have a body that takes orders from you.** It means you can appear at will. Just for the fun of it, get up out of your chair right now and go over to the light switch. Observe how electricity, **which you cannot see**

---

*Luke 1:11   †Luke 22:43   ‡Heb. 1:14

with your eyes, suddenly puts on form — LIGHT. That's what light is, you know. The manifesting of unseen energy. Now you get the idea, don't you? We are unseen spirit-beings, but like the angels or our Lord, we will be able to manifest ourselves any time . . . anyplace. We will be able to appear at will.

When the great day of our appearing comes, we will be exactly the same **persons** we are right now. We are eternal beings and already equipped for an endless existence in the spirit-world. But in the appearing we will have bodies that are subject to the spirit. That is the glorified body and we can talk about it, because the Bible does. It is physical and we can speak of it in familiar terms. About things in the spirit-world, we know almost nothing. Hence we do not speak of them.

Delightful, isn't it. Handling these great things God has in store for us! And there are more wonderful things than these. But enough is here to dispel any terror that death might hold for any Christian. Far from being an object of dread, it ushers in the most spectacular thrill anyone has ever known. Here is exciting adventure and Satan has had the temerity to cloak it with fear. Now we can almost feel sorry for him, **his greatest weapon is gone!**

WHEN SCHOOL IS OUT

Let none who reads, think to cling to this life. It is the Christian's natural right to anticipate graduation day. We cannot be as those who have no knowledge of God's plan, for we have already begun to hear the music of heaven. To ignore what the Holy Spirit sheds on us is to be like a stone. Sun shines upon a rock, but there is nothing in it to respond to that life-giving light. We are spirit-beings and God has beamed a great symphony upon our imaginations. We are living creatures, so let us rise in response to His truth.

Ask any school kid how many days until vacation and he'll tell you. As Spring brings on warmer days, he begins to count the minutes until the last bell. And school will be out for us soon. Does it seem natural to view graduation with fear? Should one dread a promotion? This world has been our school house, that's all. And the academy of life has prepared us for better things. Let us **act differently** then, when death approaches.

Let the world cling to its pleasures, its bodies, and also all it counts as precious. Our God has granted us things that even our imaginations will not fully hold.

Let the world weep and cry. Let it cling to its pleasures, its bodies and also all it counts as precious. Our God has granted us things that even our imaginations will not fully hold. Therefore we must not behave as those who feel the end of man is dust. Christians can meet death with a shout. **A shout that shocks.** And the world is shocked when it sees God's people marching through death's door beaming like children. No one can die like a Christian. Only a Christian really knows that death is **merely the last day of school!** So look world and behold what Christians do when death arrives. Look world and see how Christians parade their assurance . . . that's next!

Chapter Four

THEY ARE
WATCHING YOU!

The little girl walked into her room to play with her pet turtle. But sadness was waiting. The turtle was lying motionless in the bottom of the bowl. Quickly she called her father. Together they concluded the poor creature was dead. What a blow. The girl began to cry out of a broken heart. And when her dad attempted to console her, nothing would help. Not even the promise of a new turtle.

But then dad had an idea. "Let's have a funeral!" She looked up from her crying. She was interested, it seemed only right to give the pet a funeral. So elaborate preparations were begun. A marker was carved from wood and a little coffin designed. The girl's interest began to mount. A resting place was located. As actual ceremony plans got under way, the girl began to forget all about her turtle. She was now busy with funeral plans. Soon it was fun. But when she went to get the turtle she met with a surprise — the legs were moving. It was alive!

Her face fell. Now she was sad again.

Her face fell. Now she was sad again. She couldn't have the funeral. All the fun and excitement was over. And do you know she wasn't the least bit glad her turtle was alive. And with that unashamed capacity for change all children have, she turned to her dad and said,

"LET'S KILL IT!"

THE CHANGED ATTITUDE

See how quickly the little girl changed her mind? That's what we're suggesting in this book. I tell the story only to show how easy it is for us to *shift our attention from tragedy to adventure.* And you can do it, too. You can replace your loss at bereavement time with something new and exciting — a shocking testimony for Jesus. Suggested here is a *change of attitude toward death and funerals.* I want you to make this shift in your mind. And when you do, you will find yourself uniquely Christian.

Allow a little time to pass between the death and the service in church and most of the grief will pass. Now grief is good. You see, when a person is amused, the body chuckles. When the soul is hurt, the body cries. There should be no attempt to hold back tears at the passing of a loved one, for this is a natural expression of hurt. It does hurt to lose a loved one. No one should try to mask that. If a parent, or a child or beloved mate should leave your side, it hurts. It takes a bit of time for that hurt to be released through the grief channel.

Let death come and strike its blow to the heart. Then, as quickly as possible, *dispose of the body and the healing will start.* That is the way we are made. You know that your body starts to heal the moment an injury occurs. This is also true of the soul. Yet if you keep opening a wound, body healing is slowed. And if you keep tearing at the soul, heart-healing is delayed too. That's why your author is the bitter enemy of heathenish funeral practice.

It is much nicer to have the earthly part done with swiftly. And wait until you see the precious wonder of a *"graduation service"* in the house of God. Not only has grief come and gone, but the fuss of a corpse-centered ceremony has been avoided. Let a sufferer bask in the sweet atmosphere of God's promises, with the body disposed of and you will see the miracle of peace. Place a grieving widow in the midst of God's people and God's Word and watch her spirit rise. See how the collective witness that her beloved has graduated into heaven's delight, is a real balm.

GRADUATION CEREMONY

Notice that I do not call it a funeral service. We ought to get away from that word. For what really takes place is a graduation ceremony. The tape has been broken at the end of the race. A shout goes up. It is a thrilling, glorious experience. No, we must not call it a funeral. What could be more thrilling than stepping across the room to meet the One Who made you!

The tape has been broken at the end of the race.

But now the service has started. It is held in the church, of course. That's where it belongs. And here come the mourners, many of them are unsaved. Can't you almost feel the Lord chuckling about that? Unsaved people coming to church because they want to attend a graduation service! They are in for a treat. They have come expecting to see people crying and agonizing as they themselves do, but they're disappointed. It is like a regular church service. A man stands and testifies of his confidence in Jesus and knows his wife is waiting for him in heaven. Parents speak out their assurance that God has done the right thing in calling a child home.

The man of God speaks. His voice rings out the glad news that we are free from the world's fears. Jesus Christ has set us free.

Then the crowd lifts its voice in song. Only the redeemed can sing like that. The man of God speaks. His voice rings out the glad news that we are free from the world's fears. Jesus Christ has set us free. *This is an emotion packed time. The unsaved hear as never before.* Words and actions witness as never before. The Word of God says we are free and the people show it. The unsaved look around the room. Where is the corpse? It has already been reverently laid aside. Where are all the flowers? Why are the walls not banked with them? Sorry, the money has been used for Christ in other ways.

The service continues, but now it has the added punch of death's emotion. The truth of God set in a scene that rocks the heart. *No one can forget a service like that.* Death is everybody's business and everyone takes it seriously. And when Jesus Christ is placed in center of it, *men have to face Him seriously too.* No one can attend such a service and remain unimpressed with the reality of Christ. No one can see Christians demonstrate their fearlessness and not be moved. No one can behold the joy of the Lord in His people at a time like this and say it is unreal.

CREMATE OR BURY?

In ancient times, the heathen nations burned the bodies of their dead. Israel did not. And some have cited this as an argument against cremation today. But if this thinking were valid, surely all Christians would now favor cremation. **The tables have turned.** Modern paganism finds elaborate burials and a tender, long, last look as the best way to say good-bye to a corpse. The more stately the funeral, the sweeter the farewell. So if the comparison argument is to hold, it would appear far more Christian to cremate than to bury.

And it is just this that is causing many saints to ask, **"What should we do — bury or cremate?"** Inasmuch as the Bible has nothing to say on the subject, the question continually arises. Pagan abuses are so shocking and glaring now, strong Christians are ready to break with tradition.

Actually, there is very little difference between the two. Centuries ago they didn't know this, of course. But whether a body is placed in the ground or in an oven, the very **same process of oxidation** takes place. In the ground it occurs **slowly** and in an oven it is **fast. The only difference is time.**

 If a casket is air-tight and then placed in a protective concrete box, which is further sealed, the body can be preserved for a time. But if people are trying to preserve bodies, then perhaps the whole business of **mummies ought to be reconsidered.** But is it a matter of preservation? Is that what we are trying to do? Nowhere does the Bible even hint that we should preserve these bodies once we are through with them. To do so is the **worst form of paganism.** Why this clinging to a dead body when the Bible promises a brand new one? If a person is ready to accept the truth of the new body, then the matter becomes one of **disposal,** not **preservation!** This is no artificial distinction. Disposing of a dead body is just the opposite from trying to preserve it.

If we can agree that dead bodies are to be disposed of, then it becomes a matter of **HOW** the disposal should be carried out. It can follow sensible lines. It would seem that for those who die at sea, burial at sea is best. For those who already own cemetery property, or have access to it cheaply, burial would be best. And if cemetery property is not owned and a crematory is nearby, then cremation would be perfectly proper.

Usually it is cheaper to cremate. But if people wish to embalm their guilt feelings with a cash atonement, the bill can run as high as any burial program. Some crematories are getting fancy and then there are ornate urns and niches. But perhaps the hardest problem in connection with cremation is the fact that there are only a few hundred of them in the country today. They are not located in every state and community. If a body has to be shipped for a distance of several hundred miles, it could be more expensive, for two train tickets are required.

SO WHAT IS BEST?

 The cheapest, of course. But here is what I mean. When a death occurs, ask for the **minimum service.** Get the price before anyone gets the body. Be sure to tell the funeral director you want him only to pick up the body and either bury it or cremate it. What you are asking for is a price to dispose of the body. Often it is best to call your pastor first. He may know of a funeral director who will work with you. Should an **unscrupulous mortician** get his hands on the body, it could cost a lot of money even though previous arrangements had been made.

Now some will perform the services you want for around $200. There is no ceremony at the funeral home, no lying in state, no processions to the

90

cemetery and no limousine services. A cooperative director can pare the costs way down. He will simply dispose of the body as quickly as he can.

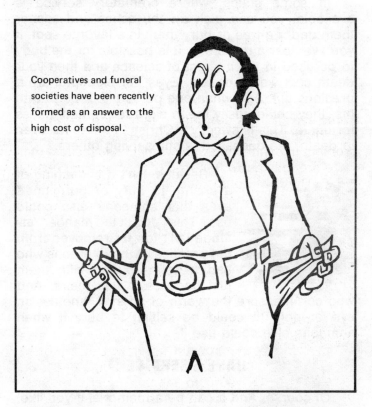

Cooperatives and funeral societies have been recently formed as an answer to the high cost of disposal.

Recently, cooperatives and funeral societies have been formed in different areas as an answer to the high cost. And some enterprising Christians have gone so far as to organize their own, with most receiving support from the larger denominations. The Los Angeles Funeral Society, for example, has contracts with local mortuaries for body disposal as low as $160.00 for burial or for cremation. This cremation price includes picking up the body and caring for all steps in the disposal process. The burial price does not include the ground. It costs

$10.00 for an entire family to join this society and that is a one time fee.

In some states, where crematory service is available, you can pick up the ashes and scatter them under a tree or bury them in a favorite spot. If you live near a university, it is possible for the body to be used in the interest of science and then your death cost would be low. Eyes, for example, are a precious gift. And when one person is through with his, they could easily mean sight for someone less fortunate. This is sweetly a Christian thing, for even in death, the deceased is still serving others.

 Besides, isn't it something of a shame to bury or burn good eyes that someone else could use? This "dog in the manger" attitude isn't too far removed from the practice of the pharaohs who had treasure buried with them just because it was theirs. And who can measure the worth of an eye! Whether an eye or gold, it could be selfish to bury it when someone else could use it.

HAVE A SERVICE

Of course. And it can be a memorial if you like. Memorials look backward, however, not forward. And it is in the future that the real excitement lies. If you can possibly avoid it, don't have the service in a funeral home. It dignifies the burying business with your sorrow. The funeral home is a fine provision for pagans and all those who otherwise feel out of place with the redeemed and in the house of God. The Christian memorial ought to be held in the church along with baptism, communion, dedications and the like. This is but the last in a precious series of lifetime events.

92

Let me say quickly that it is the **service** only, we are discussing. We are not saying Christians should never attend a pagan affair in a funeral home. This would separate us from too many wonderful opportunities to witness if we did that. It is only that we do not hold **our** services there. And this single feature can be a witness to the world. There are but few ways left in which Christians can differ from the world and this should be steadfastly maintained as one of them. It is a real testimony that no one can miss **when Christians refuse to fuss over the body** and prefer the house of God to a worldly institution.

We said the service is to honor the man, **not his body.** Actually, the writer feels it is better if **no body** were present, though he understands it is a drastic departure from custom. Not all Christians have the same passion for the future life, and some still cling to this one. Later, when they find that God cares nothing for the body, per se, they too will relegate it to its proper place. This does not mean it is to be despised. There is a sense in which God has dignified the body by placing His image within it. In that sense, it can be **referred** to discreetly, even though it may have been **disposed** of rather unceremoniously.

With the service held in the house of God, mourners arrive to pay their last respects. Then they come **under the hearing of the Gospel** in a place where the saints feel at home. They behold the people of God praising Christ and speaking of the resurrection glory. And a death can bring out unsaved people that may never have been in church before. What a sight! The exciting testimony of Christians revealing there is no death. Faces shine, lips praise God in song, and an encouraged pulpit robs death of its sting. The entire service grants reality to the truth of life after death.

The service can be much like any other church service. There is singing, prayer, maybe an offering, and then the message.

The service can be much like any other church service. There is singing, prayer, maybe an offering and then the message. The message is different, of course, **for now a Christian is being honored.** He is being feted for outstanding achievement. **He has just graduated from Phase I to Phase II.** He is being honored for receiving Christ as his personal Savior. And since the honor is for that, the future is more exciting than the past. He has moved up to higher education and the service resembles the awarding of a diploma.

It is good to honor a man of faith — for his faith! And when you do, the past life is mentioned. But it is the resurrection glory and the Lord Jesus that occupy the attention. And think of the miracle that was happening **in-side** that body! Even though that outward shell had been dying of cancer, for example, the inward man was being changed every day into the glorious image of our Lord Jesus.* This is a truth that deserves attention when a man moves up!

When my father-in-law was dying, I knelt beside his bed. He had cancer of the throat and in the last stages he couldn't speak. But he could hear. And I would talk to him about the miracle that was being produced inside his wasting body. He would squeeze my hand to tell me he understood. It was a precious truth to him and the glory of it would show through the lines of pain on his face. How I rejoiced, for even though he was my father-in-law, he was my own spiritual son in the Lord. Death was easy for him.

What a shock for non-believers to see death the Christian way. How they stagger at the sight of people actually rejoicing because a brother or sister has been promoted. What they have dreaded as a curse, they find others regarding an exciting experience. And isn't it? What can match the thrill of meeting Jesus face to face? So why shouldn't Christians praise the Lord? Death's terror has been turned to glory! And promotions are always great!

OTHER BLESSINGS

When the service, memorial or graduation type,

_____
* 2 Cor. 4:16

is held in the house of God, there are precious side benefits. At once, the **unholy** practice of squandering money on a corpse is avoided. And those who love the Lord regret that some Christians will lavish funds on a corpse they wouldn't spend for a servant on the mission field. This is deplorable and there will be an accounting for the abuse at the judgment.

 Money saved through avoiding the commercial funeral could go into a Christian project. And if all Christians followed the **principle of disposal,** huge sums could be salvaged. But for the family in need, the saving would be a great blessing. It can take years to recover from a $2000 funeral where the means are limited. And pastors are very understanding about this. Usually the church building is available without charge and pastors are happy to serve in their own pulpits. No flowers are needed, except a spray or bouquet to mark the scene.

In my own pastorate, we use the regular Sunday service for the "graduations." If a death occurs during the week, the body is disposed of the quickest and cheapest way. And then on Sunday, the regular worship service is held in the name of the deceased. If more time is needed to notify distant relatives and allow for notices, the service can be held a week later. But the Sunday service fits everyone's schedule. No one has to leave his work to attend. No one has an excuse for not coming. And so the "graduation" is a huge success. Crowds come under the preaching of the word and the time is not begrudged.

HOW DOES GOD FEEL ABOUT IT?

When Christians show attention to the soul rather

than the body, God is delighted. They are beginning to think as He does. Did not Jesus teach, **"Fear not them which can kill the body and do no more. . . ?"** And when it comes to disposing of the body, some might ask what God thinks of burial and cremation. Honestly, God couldn't care less. He was concerned with it only as long as a man was in it. For **only then** was it the temple of the Holy Spirit.

When bodies are occupied by people, He cares very much about them. They are a part of our stewardship. We are expected to take care of them and dedicate them to His service. But once they have been abandoned, they are of no use to Him or us any longer. And if one were to ask Him directly what should be done with the body, or, what HE would do about it, likely He would answer: **"Well, what do I do with things when I am through with them?"** And if you know your Bible you'll say: **"Burn them."** And He'd answer, **"Well. . . .?"**

When God is through with this world He will burn it. He says so. To Him it is like a blood-soaked bandage and the best place for that is the fire. It makes sense. Consider all the people who have paraded across the stage beginning with the first man. These have died and their carcasses have left this world a huge burial ground. Billions of bodies have made this globe a giant cemetery. It should be burned. And what of the bodies that fill the earth? They will be cremated by God's own hand, **making any fuss over burial or cremation pointless.** God is going to cremate the whole business with one blast.*

---

* 2 Peter 3:10-12

PREPARATION

Death and taxes are unavoidable.

"Death and taxes are unavoidable." You've heard that plenty of times. And you know it's true. So **determine ahead of time** to avoid the barbaric ordeal of a big public funeral with its temptation toward outward show. You will find you can maintain your own Christian spirit much easier where attention is focused on eternal life, rather than a flower laden casket.

Bereavement is coming, so prepare to accept it as one who has eternal life and know that, even while you suffer, God has healing for the deepest human hurt. Look to the Everlasting Arms rather than the ceremonies of men and you won't be disappointed. Bear your loss with serenity and without complaint, for Jesus does all things well. Stand erect as a witness for Christ in a world that judges us not so much by **what we say,** as by **how we act** in the crises of life.

Maintain your testimony by separating yourself from the world's tragic hold on the flesh and be a shock for Christ! Let the world see your contempt for paganism. Let bereavement time be a triumphant hour. And with other Christians joining in, soon death itself can produce that kind of saltness that will make us the seasoning of earth! And it is easy, when we **plan ahead.**

A bereavement is coming. Your pastor may know of a funeral director who works with people interested in disposal only. And if he doesn't, then join a funeral society that gives you protection ahead of time. The cost is surprisingly low since the societies enter into contract arrangements for **minimum** services. But don't wait until death arrives!

In a grief stricken condition, you are like no other buyer. If you were in need of a home or new car, you would shop for the best deal. At least you would have some idea as to what you wanted and should pay. But the funeral buyer is in no mood to compare prices and his decision is generally an on-the-spot one. The soft-spoken mortician says just sign here and we'll take care of everything. **And then it is too**

late. The victim, Christian or not, is caught up in the burial tradition and it is expensive.

So plan ahead and be ready. With the body business all settled you will be able to concentrate on your testimony for Jesus at bereavement time. But if it isn't you will be thrown off balance. That body will concern you so much, you will find yourself behaving like the heathen. And this warning is given in all sincerity, please take it seriously.

Only Christians can laugh at death.

Before us is a whole new approach to the Christian witness and a time when it can be most effective. Only Christians can laugh at death and this needs to be exploited for Christ. You may think what is suggested here is too revolutionary and that you would have to change your entire outlook on the body to go along with it. But you must, dear reader. Those who take a stand for Jesus should never be afraid to break with tradition. Virile Christianity is always revolutionary!

We are a different people and we must do things differently from the world. If you want to count for Christ at a time when **eyes are on you,** then you will take heed to death, the Christian way. Don't let the fear of what people will think, prevent you from standing out for Christ. And you can do it. You may think you can't, but you can.

We live in a world that is more interested in what Christians **DO** than in what they say. The radio waves are crowded with good sermons and TV is following the same path. Great evangelists rise and the crowds hear. But it is **demonstrated Christianity** that affects people, not uttered truths. And the present moral decline is taking place in the face of the best preaching and with 50% of America going to church. Obviously, no one is paying attention to what is being said. And why should they, when Christians behave no differently from anyone else? Until the spoken word is dramatized and vindicated by God's people, it is meaningless.

THE DIFFERENCE IN DEATH

Please don't think it strange that I suggest the church be different in death! It may be the last stronghold of Christian uniqueness. The world has pushed us almost to the grave and we have to take a last stand. Christianity is dying out, as far as

an effective witness is concerned. And if she is going to regain her difference, she will have to start now. And the matter of dying is one place it can really count.

Here is the thing the heathen fear most. If Christians can demonstrate their fearlessness here, the world will be impressed. And in the same moment, the truth of Christ and the resurrection will be dramatized and reinforced. And to do it, we will have to **break with the world and its tradition.** And we'd better, before it robs us of our vitality and virility completely.

But you can't be different unless Christ has taken a real hold on your life. Nowhere else do we show the slender grasp of our Savior as in the wantonness of our grief and surprise at the death of a loved one. We almost act as if they should not die and were given to us to defend against time. But, is there no one else who loves them? Are we to use our love as chains and bonds that we might bind them to earth? If Jesus has a real hold on your life, then do not squander the opportunity to honor Him, by covering your sorrow with an expensive atonement.

Start thinking now how the death of a loved one can be used to impress the world for Christ. You will see God's power as you do. And when bereavement strikes; let your first thought be, **"How will I use this for Jesus!"** Then see how any idea of personal loss fades into the joy of honoring our Lord. Why, just the thought of bringing glory to our Master can replace much of what hurts the soul. And when the world sees you happy **at a funeral** — it will taste the uniqueness of Christianity!

When God calls someone from your side, don't waste the opportunity in self-indulgent pity. And don't throw it away on foolish ceremonialism. That is for the heathen. **They are in the dark.** Oh, how they would love to find you in the wailing room. And they expect to see a body out there with a preacher eulogizing the dead man. That is their tradition and they want you to do it too. How pleased they are when you follow the hearse to the cemetery and there's another sad scene at the graveside. That's what they do. However, that would be putting your seal of approval on their behavior. And they want that so badly. They feel better when Christians do things their way.

The people who built America were tough. They loved Jesus and were willing to honor Him.

Be a rebel and see if it doesn't make you feel warm inside. Don't you think it is worth fighting to preserve our uniqueness? Of course, you do. In a sense we are fighting for the very existence of our

Christian witness. God has called us to be different and we must be so different the world will slam on the brakes and do a double-take. The people who built America were tough. Their manners were not so polished, but they loved Jesus and were willing to honor Him. They were different. But they were rebels.

If you will join the fight for Christian uniqueness you will soon forget all your own cares and anxieties. You will toss aside any personal fears and conflicts and an amazing spiritual health will sweep over you as you join in the battle of being different for Christ. This is a big fight. The funeral people will not like it. But it will make you big to be a part of it. And your life will become exciting in the process.

So parade your fearlessness of death. Let the heathen be shocked. Now is the time. Oh sure, some will say, **"It's not dignified,"** or **"It doesn't seem right somehow."** They are in the dark. Laugh in the face of the funeral mongers who tell you it doesn't show proper respect and seems goulish. They only want to perpetuate the tradition that is making them rich. But praise the Lord! When Christ sets us free, it is from the rudiments of this world. We are no longer bound by the traditions of men. And the insights of this book can let you say to the fearful, **"There's nothing to it."**

This is the way Christian uniqueness can be restored to the church. People coming away from such a service will either want that fearlessness for themselves or simply marvel at the wonder of Christianity. **But they have noticed the difference.** And when all our Christians and churches shift to this attitude, America will be shocked by the difference. This is not a preached Gospel only, **now it is demonstrated.** It is when God puts a difference between His people and those around them, that they are unique. And without that difference they have nothing. Let Christians display their joy in death and the world will be shocked! They will be God's peculiar people once more.

DEATH—"GRADUATION DAY"

Some years ago my father-in-law went to be with Jesus. I was kneeling beside his bed just hours before his departure. He couldn't speak. Cancer made his jaw immovable. But he could faintly squeeze my hand and blink his eyes. I asked him if he was looking forward to seeing Jesus. His eyes lit up and his hand trembled. I sensed he was trying to tell me something. The Holy Spirit led me to ask,

> "Hal, are you trying to tell me you are anxious to get out of this body and on to the great things Jesus has for you?"

With his remaining strength, he squeezed my hand vigorously. I found myself actually shaking hands with him. It took me a moment to realize the Spirit of God was prompting me to congratulate a man who was about to "graduate."

Shortly he was gone. All that was left was a dead body, one full of disease. What should we do with it? Hal was through with it. So was the Holy Spirit. None of us wanted it for anything. Since the arrangement had been taken care of in advance, I made the one phone call. The body was taken away and we never saw it again. That was a blessing, believe me.

• A few days later we had the service here at our

105

PC chapel. It was NOT a funeral service, neither was it a memorial. It was a *"graduation"* service. After all, Hal had done the greatest thing a man can do — receive Christ as his Savior. Thus his future was far more exciting than his past had ever been. So instead of looking back, which funerals do, we honored him for being in Christ and what that meant to his future. "Graduation" was the only word that fit the situation.

It seems only proper that Christians should be regarded as "graduates."

SINCE THEN

We've never had a funeral at PC. But we have had any number of "graduation" services. As friends and relatives of PC members have gone to be with Jesus, we have honored them for passing through this one life and succeeding in the one thing God asks of all men — receive Christ. This makes them well prepared to enter the next life. Therefore death makes them "graduates" in the truest sense. While funerals might be fitting for the unsaved, it seems only proper that Christians should be regarded as "graduates." For that is exactly what they are.

Chapter Five

CONSIDER NOW

1. **PLAN AHEAD** Probably the real sin of bereavement is waiting until a death occurs before doing anything about arrangements. And when it does come, you will be in no condition to think straight. You could then find yourself forced into an impulsive decision that will sweep you into the corpse-centered, status-symbol type funeral that is just the opposite of death, the Christian way.

2. Talk with your pastor to see if he has contact with a mortician that will perform minimum burial or cremation services. If he does, then be sure to get your pre-need instructions on file with that mortician. Then, when death strikes, one phone call takes care of everything. This will free you to concentrate on your Christian

witness. It is a good idea to leave a copy on file with your pastor too.

3. Investigate the protections of the nearest funeral society. Don't delay in this. It could save you a lot of money as well as severe anxiety.

4. Start thinking in terms of **disposal,** rather than **preservation.** Once you do, the false trimming of a "decent burial" will be stripped away. There is absolutely nothing respectable about a dead body. The viewing of embalmed remains is rare outside the United States and Canada.

5. If a death should catch you unprepared, don't panic. A body will keep for about 24 hours. This gives you time to make arrangements, but it will be stressful for you. A salesman will lead you about the funeral parlor all the while counselling in a sympathetic tone. And you will be tortured with thoughts, **"I must do the right thing. This is no time for me to be selfish and think of money. What will people think?"** You can see that your judgment will be poor.

6. Funeral people often confuse facts with fiction when it appears a sale is likely and a severely stressed prospect is on the hook. It helps to know that:

   a. Embalming is not necessary. No state requires it, except in special circumstances where the body is going to be shipped by public carrier, or where there is a communicable disease.

   b. No casket is required for cremation (Calif. Law). Though they may imply that it is. Most crematoriums have material on hand for that purpose and it is included in the $80 charged

109

for cremation. Some private crematoriums will not cremate without one, because they are in the casket-selling business themselves.

c. No vault is required by law in most states. Cemeteries like to sell these to prevent the ground from settling after the coffin disintegrates. They will try to get you to buy one for about $120.

7. Burial is as repugnant as cremation. An exhumed, embalmed body is a sickening, grotesque sight. It would be a fantastic error to refer to it as the image of a promoted Christian. Even the most expensive casket will disintegrate. And a sealed one is worse than an unsealed one, for in it thrive the putrefactive bacteria and the results of their growth are horrible. A body is better off with no casket at all.*

8. Don't witness a cremation. The repulsiveness of a body decomposing in the ground is almost matched by one being oxidized in a furnace. The real advantage lies in the ashes being disposed of easier than a body. And of course, it puts an end to all arguments about health, sanitation and cemetery care.

9. Cemetery prices vary greatly. If you decide on burial, check on the price of space in the outlying districts and suburban areas. Often you can find them for about $150 including opening and closing costs. If you join a funeral society, they will have already been checked out for you.

---

* Dr. Jesse Carr, Chief of Pathology at San Francisco General Hospital and Professor of Pathology at U.C. Medical School.

10. Leave instructions for disposal of your body. Let your family know your wishes with respect to your body. Where your will specifies your body is to be used for scientific research, the survivors are bound to carry out the directions.

Plan on some kind of death or burial insurance.

11. Plan on some kind of death or burial insurance that will give the family a little help when you are promoted. Sometimes a short trip is a good aid in making the readjustment. And the insurance payment could cover it.

12. Life insurance is practical for Christians. Those who work for a living, thank God for their daily bread. And those who benefit from an insurance policy will do the same. Every good thing a Christian receives brings praise to God, even though the Lord used a human means to produce it.

"but if any provide not for his own, and specially for those of his own house, he hath denied the faith and is worse than an infidel." *

NOTE: There are funeral and memorial societies all over the United States who can direct you to mortuaries cooperating with the pre-need (disposal) plan I have outlined in this book. Contact: The Continental Association of Funeral and Memorial Societies, 1828 L Street NW, Washington, DC 20036. They will send you a list of these societies and you can contact the one nearest you and receive a lot of helpful information.

IN LIEU OF FLOWERS

Some Christians are reluctant to waste God's money on flowers for a funeral. They only last a few days. Some funeral sprays are expensive. If you have a relative or friend who passes away and it is expected that you will pay your respects in the form of flowers or some other token, you may be happy to learn of a service that Personal Christianity is ready to provide for you.

Instead of using that money for flowers, you may send it to us here at PC as an offering for the ministry. We have prepared a lovely Christian Memorial Acknowledgment which we will send to the bereaved family in your name. They will appreciate the fact that you have made a LIVING MEMORIAL for their loved one. It will NOT show the amount of your gift, but simply say that a GENEROUS gift has been made for the spreading of the gospel of our Lord Jesus Christ. This will express your love to the bereaved family in a spiritual way.

Turn to pages 136-138 for a picture of the acknowledgment and its message.

---

* 1 Tim. 5:8

112

(sample of the pre-need form your mortician will give you)

Funeral Instructions

For the purpose of relieving _____My Wife_____ of the burden of making decisions
(Closest Relative)
and arrangements in the event of need, I herewith execute definite instructions regarding my funeral
services.

1. I wish my funeral to be public ☐ private ☐   NO FUNERAL

2. I wish the services to be held at_____

3. I have viewed caskets and would prefer_____

4. I have viewed vaults and would prefer_____

5. I wish my funeral expense to total_____and to include_____
   _____minimum_____
   _____
   _____
   _____

6. I desire_____clothing and prefer_____color.
   (New or Your Own)

7. My preference for burial arrangements is as follows :_____
   _____cremation_____
   _____

8. My church affiliation is_____

9. I would prefer as clergyman_____

10. I wish the following music_____

11. Other instructions or remarks :_____
    _____All services to be held in my church_____
    _____
    _____
    _____

WITNESSES:

_____   *C. S. Lovett*
                                (Signature—Full Name)
_____

113

Chapter Six

WITNESSING AND DEATH

Death — the great intruder.

When I was a boy the man at the corner gas station often befriended me. He'd let me fill my bicycle tires with his air hose. Later, when I had my own jalopy, he'd sometimes fill the tank with gas. One day I went to the station and he didn't come out to greet me. That was unusual. I walked around to the back of his shop. There he was, seated on a box leaning against the wall. His lunch pail was in his lap. But he wasn't eating. In fact, he didn't move. I drew closer. Then I gasped — **he was dead.** Apparently he had suffered a stroke and died instantly. What a chilling discovery.

I backed away. That discovery changed everything — fast. The family came. The ambulance people arrived. The station was closed. Sad faces were everywhere. What a shock. My friend was gone and now everything was different. Death is the great intruder. That event changed my routine and the entire way of life for his family.

Now why do I tell that? Only that we might again consider how death is so dramatic that it grips the soul and imagination of everyone involved. Why do I speak of it here? To ask this: shouldn't we use something as compelling as death to draw people's attention to Christ? Isn't it a matter of wisdom to take the traumas and dramas of life and USE THEM for Jesus? Shouldn't we use everything we can, big or little, as a witness for the Lord?

IS THAT IDEA NEW TO YOU?

Consider the words of the apostle Paul: "Whatsoever you do in word or deed, do all in the name of the Lord Jesus. . . ." (Col. 3:17). Did you know that our lives are not our own to use as we please? That's right. When we take Jesus as our Savior and receive the gift of eternal life, we belong to Him. Our bodies become temples of the Holy Spirit and we are no longer our own (Ist Cor. 6:19). The Lord owns us lock, stock and barrel. He says further that those in Christ must, "no longer live for themselves, but for Him Who died for them" (2 Cor. 5:15).

If we're wise we'll learn to harness every area of our lives for Jesus. In one place the Lord said, "The sons of this world are more shrewd in relation to their own kind than are the sons of light" (Luke 16:8). By that He

115

meant, the people of this world are quicker to exploit the opportunities for getting ahead in this world, than believers are in getting ahead in the next. He is exhorting Christians to wake up and start taking advantage of the opportunities that come their way. You see it is just as necessary to work and plan to get ahead in the next life as it is in this one. There is no way to make it big IN CHRIST without applying yourself.

Now if the idea of using DEATH as a witness for Jesus is new to you, then it is probable that you have never been informed that we are to use all the areas of our lives in witnessing for Christ. I want you to consider it now. If the Holy Spirit affirms that you are safe in Jesus, then He will also tell you that you are called to invest yourself in His service. The one clear command which He has given to us all is this: "Ye shall be witnesses unto me. . . ." (Acts. 1:8). To be a witness for Christ one must know **how to harness** the routine of his life and make it count for the Lord.

THAT'S OUR MINISTRY

See that book. The title is **Witnessing Made Easy.** It contains 256 pages of witnessing know-how. It will introduce you to the **ladder-method** of witnessing. And you are going to thrill to it, especially if you tend to be shy and it is hard for you to speak to strangers about the Lord. It is a ten step plan that ASSUMES most Christians are timid at first. That's what makes it attractive to those who don't like to be thrown into a situation where they have to sink or swim.

You know about ladders, don't you?

Just as a man cannot go from the ground to the roof of his house without a ladder, neither can a Christian go from silence to active witnessing without a plan which breaks the distance up into easy steps.

Here's a man who wants to get to the roof of his house. He eyes the distance. It's at least 12 feet. Can he make it in one jump? Of course not. So what does he do? He goes and gets a ladder. He leans it against the house and what he couldn't do in one single bound, he does very easily ONE STEP AT A TIME.

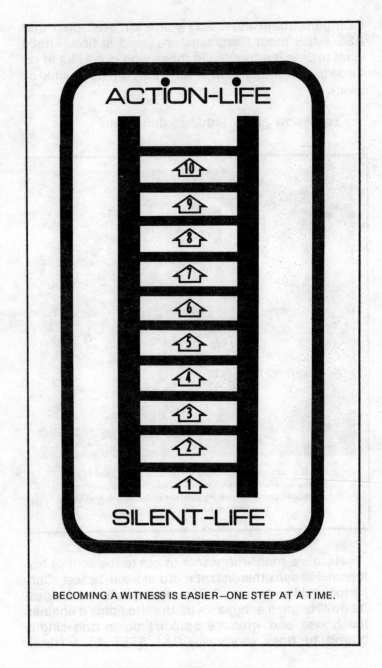

ACTION-LIFE

10
9
8
7
6
5
4
3
2
1

SILENT-LIFE

BECOMING A WITNESS IS EASIER—ONE STEP AT A TIME.

Each rung takes him that much higher until he is finally where he wants to be — on top of his house.

So it is with the ladder-method of witnessing. You are not expected to go right out and start talking to people about Jesus. You start at the bottom, in situations where you have no direct contact with people at all. Then you work your way gradually to the place where it is easy and natural for you to share your faith with others. To expect you to become a witness in ONE JUMP is ridiculous. We don't do anything else in life that way. Why should we expect to do so with the things of the Lord.

Then — as you work your way up the ladder, you learn how to use ALL the areas of your life as a witness for Jesus. It doesn't matter whether it is a trip to the store, or someone calls at your door, you're already and you know exactly what to do.

HERE'S THE FIRST STEP

If I describe the first action for you, you'll get an idea how the Lord can use such a plan to build your strengths as a witness.

We'll assume you have gone to a gas station. While the attendant is putting gas in your car, you visit the restroom. You are going to leave a tract there, but this time it will be different from anything you have done before. You go inside the restroom. "Click," you lock the door. Now there is no way for anyone to surprise you as you do the action I am about to describe. This is the ideal way to start off as a witness for the Lord — **in the world.** It's easy to testify for him in church, but out there in the world it is another story.

Let your palm linger over your heart. Feel that accelerated heartbeat?

Your hand reaches to your shirt pocket for a tract. But don't take it out just yet. Let your palm linger over your heart. Feel that accelerated heartbeat? Kerplump ... kerplump ... kerplump ...? Why so fast? Ah — you're about to do something for Jesus in the world. That's Satan's territory! Even though the door is locked you are still in the place of fear. It's scary witnessing for the Lord — in the world.

Now you can bring out the tract. Hold it at arm's length. See it flutter? Why does it shake so? That's the trembling of your heart translated into something you can see. It's good to realize we have this fear. It's also good to know what to do about it. With your arm still outstretched, speak to the Holy Spirit. "God the Holy Spirit, behold my trembling heart and comfort me now!"

120

"Holy Spirit, behold my trembling heart and comfort me now!"

Look at your tract now. See — it settles down. The work of the Holy Spirit is now translated into something you can see! And what do you feel in your heart? Glorious comfort. Isn't that great! You're not through yet. Say aloud . . . **"In the name of the Lord Jesus Christ,"** and let your arm swing so that you deposit the tract on a shelf or towel box. That little exercise may seem overly simple to you, but I assure you it is a fabulous way to begin your career as a witness for Jesus. It is no small thing to have Jesus' Name on your lips in a public place.

We all have to start some place. How better than by sampling the Spirit's power in a situation that offers minimum threat. You've just seen how it is done. That's only the beginning. Imagine what the rest of the steps are like. As you climb the ladder you will learn dozens of new ways to use tracts and create witnessing opportunities. At the top of the ladder you will be able to turn almost ANY conversation into a witnessing situation. What a witness your life will become! In fact, if you want to, you can go on and learn a plan for winning souls. You'll have the strength for it. But until he climbs the ladder, there's not one Christian in a hundred who has the personality strength to present Christ to a stranger. This method of witnessing brings that kind of strength.

Say aloud..."In the name of the Lord Jesus Christ."

What you are going to like most is learning to work with the Holy Spirit — at close range. This is vital, for it is HE Who shows you how to use your life as a witness for the Lord Jesus. It is going to thrill you to watch the Spirit work right before your eyes as you do the various actions described in this course. Once you begin, you'll ask yourself, "Why didn't I start this a long time ago?" Now listen to the testimony of someone who has learned the ladder-method of witnessing:

Susan Mele praises the Lord for what He has done in her life through the WITNESSING COURSE.

"When I look back to 18 months ago when I first started this course, I chuckle as I think how afraid I was of people. I can't help but praise the Lord for what He has done in my life through you people. I have never had so much fun with anything before. The real thrill has been working with the Holy Spirit. I certainly am not through. I have just begun to use my life for the Lord. Yet, I can honestly say that if I went no farther, this course was more than worthwhile for me. I have a lot of precious memories from doing the exercises since I was 'salvaged from silence!' I am recommending this course to everyone who will listen to my story!"

Susan L. Mele
13038 Dorothy Drive
Chesterland, OH 44026   (used by permission)

Isn't that terrific! I have hundreds of letters like that from people who have been lifted to a new level in Christ. Most confess they didn't realize there were so many ways to use the ordinary incidents of their daily routine for Christ. Don't you think you should send for a copy of *Witnessing Made Easy* and see what this method could do for your life? Perhaps another word of encouragement would help. Listen to the testimony of Raymond J. Weaverling, 18 Rankin Rd., Meeting House Hill, Newark, DE 17911:

Raymond Weaverling has witnessed to all his neighbors and has given out more than 3,000 tracts!

"It thrills me to look back to where I was when I first started up the ladder. Why, I was afraid to give a tract to a stranger. Even the thought of having someone see me leave a tract some place was too much for me. But the Lord has used you and this course to change all that, praise His name! I have witnessed to all my neighbors and have given out more than 3000 tracts! The fear of what people might think has left me. I never dreamed that a person could CREATE witnessing opportunities as I do now. This really is a fantastic course and I commend it to Christians everywhere!"

(used by permission)

How about it? Are you ready to let the Lord show you ways to use your life as a witness for Him? Are you ready to learn ways to witness of which you never dreamed? I hope so. Take my word for it, there is no way to know the real thrill of Christ unless we obey Him and learn how to move in the power of His Spirit. That's what makes the Christian life exciting. And the best way to begin that kind of excitement is to get active as a witness.

ABOUT THE AUTHOR. . .DR. C. S. LOVETT

Dr. Lovett is the president of **Personal Christianity,** a fundamental, evangelical interdenominational ministry. For the past 27 years he has had but one objective—**preparing Christians for the second coming of Christ!** This book is one of over 35 of his works designed to help believers be **prepared for His appearing.**

Dr. Lovett's decision to serve the Lord resulted in the loss of a sizable personal fortune. He is well equipped for the job the Lord has given him. A graduate of California Baptist Theological Seminary, he holds the M.A. and B.D. degrees conferred *Magna Cum Laude.* He has also completed graduate work in psychology at Los Angeles State College and holds an honorary doctorate from the Protestant Episcopal University in London.

A retired Air Force Chaplain (Lt. Colonel), he has been married to Marjorie for over 36 years and has two grown daughters dedicated to the Lord.

Would you like to see a copy of the message I deliver at our graduation services? You'll find a copy reproduced on the following pages. That way you can tear it out if you like. Why not show it to your pastor? It's possible that he will agree that bodies should be disposed of rather than honored. He may give thought to holding a "graduation" service in his church. Such a service can be just as emotion packed as any funeral, but the truth of Christ and the fact the believer is still alive rings out as never before. Imagine the effect this could have on unsaved mourners who come to your church to pay their "last respects" to the graduate. Naturally, you will feel free to change the message to make it fit your style of presentation and your situation.

"GRADUATION DAY"

Funeral Sermon

INTRODUCTION

Today we dedicate this service to _____
But not to his memory! This is not a memorial service entirely, for memorials look back and honor the past life only. We are concerned with the future of _____ as well. And what we are doing here today is very much akin to those ceremonies that honor men for outstanding achievement.

We are honoring _____ for outstanding achievement. He has done the highest thing a man can do, that is receive Jesus Christ as his personal Savior. And since we are honoring him for that, we are more concerned about his future than his past. When a person receives Christ, the future is changed. His whole destiny is reshaped. The future, you see, is far more exciting now than the past could ever be. So you will find this service very different. It is not a funeral and it is not really a memorial. It is a dedication service and we are honoring a **person.**

DEATH—A CHRISTIAN EXPERIENCE

There is nothing sadder than a heathen funeral. And by heathen I do not mean those born in darkest Africa or one who is not a religious person. Don't be surprised if I tell you our churches are well attended by heathen. A heathen, to me, is anyone who does not know Christ, personally. And the reason the heathen funeral is so sad? Well, what comfort can you give?

I must say this, though. It is fitting to hold funerals for non-Christians. For them, you see, the memory of the past is the more beautiful. The future brings only judgment and terror. These people must cling to memories, so all is crowded into a sad funeral and they say "goodbye forever." No expense is spared; they can't do enough; it is a farewell splurge. We do not deny them this. Likely this earth is all the heaven they will ever know and it is fitting indeed that a sad ceremony mark the occasion.

But can it be like that for the Christian? No, it can never be like that for one who has already walked with the Lord. And so there is no body here (optional). We are not honoring the form in which _____ lived, but we are honoring him. God has already honored the body by putting _____ in it. Its job is finished and we have returned it to the dust of which it was moulded. This we have done quietly and discreetly. And even now we commit it to the earth.

But this is not to say we feel no loss or pain.

130

Indeed we do. Our hearts are saddened, of course. We miss good friends. And if they are only boarding a plane for a trip, their absence produces a hurt. Yes, we feel that. And there will be that vacancy until we are together again. But that won't be long. There is a lot to do in the meantime. Before we know it, we will be joined, again.

But how different when it is like today. This is a Christian experience. Our brother _____ was a Christian. He knew Jesus as his personal Savior. And I have had a number of talks with him about the truth of God. I knew his heart. So, far from being a depressing time, this is not a no-hope funeral. Instead of looking on death as something of horror and tragedy, we can give our attention to the glory and marvel of it.

GLORY OF DEATH!

God has never intended for man to spend much time on the earth. The whole process of being on earth is one of death. The minute we are born we begin to die. Some sooner and some later. Death is the chief character of things physical. When a man is born he arrives in a dying world. Even the sun is going out, scientists tell us. And this huge ball on which we live is little more than a huge cemetery. Christians know this. This is why they are reluctant to get too involved with it. They find life on earth to be a very temporary thing and consider that the big story of man lies after death.

Christians also know something else. Man is not a body. He merely has a body which he occupies for a time. And that body is an animal body. The man himself who lives inside that body is a spirit-being, like God. God is a Spirit, the Bible tells us, and since man is the image of God, He is made in the image of a Spirit. And spirits can live in any kind of a body or they can live without one.

Death, to the Christian, is little more than changing clothes. The very same person sheds this body and gets a new one. There is no change in the person. He is not affected by this change of clothes at all. But the new body he acquires is more suited to living in the Spirit and in the presence of Jesus. Naturally the old one is left behind. It cannot serve the image of God where he goes.

This does not mean that no one should be afraid of death. Indeed there are those who should fear it. And all men, without Christ, fear it, because they are sinners. You can understand how there would be an unconscious dread of meeting God, can't you? Men with their guilts fear judgment and punishment. And without any light on the subject, instinctively they feel that it lies beyond death. And they should, until they receive Christ!

Then it all changes. The total forgiveness that God gives us through Christ, removes this dread. And because it is very real, it erases the fear of judgment. So now, by faith, we are able to set aside our fears and any undue sorrow and behold this remarkable Christian experience!

OUR SERVICE CHANGED

We are honoring _____ today. And if he were able to present himself to us in some way right now, we would have him come forward and receive a plaque of some kind. But he is getting his plaque from more worthy hands than ours. He has gone to be honored by the Savior he loved. If we could have a remote unit set up to see it, we would be thrilled at the sight. But we don't and we will have to be content to honor him in absentia.

But if there were a remote unit set up here and he could speak to us from the monitor, he would not tell us of the glory of heaven. He would not say one word about the blows of this life and any suffering he endured. Those are his treasures now. Instead, he would speak of the amazing new life before him; his surroundings and especially of the Lord.

His voice would come out of heaven's stereo to say to us:

"I never knew Jesus was such a fabulous person. Oh, He is so wonderful. He makes me feel so important to Him, He is with me all the time. He has not once scolded me or rebuked me or made me feel small. Actually, He makes me feel as though I were the most important person in His life! It is more wonderful than I ever dreamed; I can't tell you of the joy I feel right now. There are no words. Just wait until you see Him. It isn't possible to have in the world what I have right now!"

Our ears would be straining to catch some insight to heaven's glory. We would like to know so much more. Maybe he will give some clues:

"COME BACK THERE? TO THAT LIFE? Not for a moment. Why, this is fantasy land! What peace and joy . . . I guess exultation is a better word. You can't even begin to know what it's like. And besides I have a thrilling new job, just right for me. I love it. And I wouldn't leave it for a second. No, sir. I'll wait for you . . . but hurry up. You don't know what you're missing!"

133

Well, we don't have any monitor set up. And _____ is not allowed to speak to us for that would violate the faith method. It just wouldn't be fair for us to have a privilege like that when the rest of the world does not. And yet there is a way in which_____ can speak to us — through me. I can speak for him. That's my job, actually. And he would have only one message for everyone here. Here it is.

> "You know that I have no wealth to distribute in a will. There wasn't too much to share. But let me tell you of a fantastic will in which we can all share! The Last will and Testament of my Savior, the Lord Jesus Christ! It is often called the New Testament. . . .

> "Under the terms of this will men can receive a priceless gift! And that gift is a Person!* And when men receive this gift, this Person, they themselves become the sons of God in that same second.† And now because I received Christ, I feel at home in the awsome majesty of God. My heart beats with unspeakable joy as I behold the beauty and wonder of this Savior of mine! And as I look across the wealth of heaven, I know that it is as much mine as His!

> "Wouldn't you like to share in this will? Won't you do as I did and say to Jesus, 'Lord, I am a sinner, I want you for my personal Savior?' I'm so glad I took Jesus as my Savior, I beg you not to pass Him by!"

Will you notice I haven't praised our brother this morning. I haven't said a word about how good or

_____

* John 3:16   † John 1:12

bad he was. You see that has nothing to do with it. The one thing he or anyone else can do to please God is to receive His Son, Jesus Christ, as Savior. That's all that _____ could do. And that is what he did!

PRAY

Committal, if any.

C. S. Lovett

CHRISTIAN MEMORIAL ACKNOWLEDGMENT

Presented below is a copy of the acknowledgment that we send in your name. You can see how the message is Christ-centered. When your friends receive this lovely card, they will understand that a generous gift has been made in the name of their loved one.

OUR

GREATEST

COMFORT...

Jesus said, "I am the resurrection, and the life; he who believes
in Me shall live even if he dies." (John 11:25)

(sample card and matching envelope at reduced size)

"A Christian Memorial"

Dear

Mrs. Mary Smith

You will be pleased to know that a generous gift
has been made to **Personal Christianity Chapel** for the
spreading of the gospel of our Lord Jesus Christ in the name of:

Allen Smith

by

Mr. and Mrs. James Jones
652 South Flower
Los Angeles, California 90026

The Lord Jesus makes this invitation to all men:

"Behold I stand at the door and knock: if
any man hear my voice and open the door
. . . I will come in"   —Rev. 3:20

Because of the gift made in the name of your loved
one, this invitation will be personally carried to men and
women everywhere. They will be encouraged to answer
the Lord's knock and open their hearts to Him. When
they do, Christ becomes their personal Savior.

That's why this is a Christian Memorial.

To take advantage of this service, simply fill in the form below. Detach it from the book and mail to Personal Christianity, Box 549, Baldwin Park, CA 91706, along with the amount you wish to invest in the Lord. We will then send the card in your name. Your friends will be pleased that the money was not spent on flowers, etc., but went into something that could serve as a living memorial. Yes, your gift is tax deductible.

If you do not want to cut up your book, simply put the same information below in a letter to us.

■ ■ ■ ■ ■ ■ CLIP AND MAIL THIS PORTION ■ ■ ■ ■ ■ ■

PERSONAL CHRISTIANITY
Box 549, Baldwin Park, CA 91706

(PLEASE TYPE OR PRINT PLAINLY)

Dear brethren, I wish to make a Christian Memorial in the amount of $ _____

☐ Please send me an offering receipt.

This gift is in memory of:_____

Please send a Memorial Acknowledgment Card to:

Name _____

Address _____

City_____State _____Zip_____

Memorial given by:

Name _____

Address _____

City_____State_____Zip_____

PERSONAL CHRISTIANITY

BOX 549, BALDWIN PARK,
CALIFORNIA 91706
(213) 338-7333

SINCE 1951

QUICK ORDER FORM

PRINT PLAINLY SO PRAYER GROUP CAN PROPERLY READ YOUR NAME. | 7502

NAME_____

EACH TIME YOU ORDER, PLEASE USE EXACT SAME NAME

ADDRESS_____

CITY_____ STATE_____ ZIP _____

ITEM NO.	TITLE	HOW MANY	COST EACH	TOTAL AMOUNT

DISCOUNT SCHEDULE		
if your order totals:	**TOTAL ORDER**	
$15.00–$24.99 **subtract $1.50**	☞ **LESS DISCOUNT**	
$25.00–$49.99 **subtract $5.00**		
$50.00 or more **subtract 25%**	**NET AFTER DISCOUNT**	
SPECIAL POSTAGE	**CALIFORNIA** RESIDENTS ONLY ADD 6% SALES TAX	
☐ **SPECIAL HANDLING**		
☐ **SPECIAL DELIVERY**	**HELP ON POSTAGE**	
☐ **AIR MAIL**	**OFFERING**—help with free literature distribution	
☐ **AIR MAIL-SPEC DEL**		
Check box and enclose extra postage for above services. Amount enclosed determines shipping method.	**TOTAL AMOUNT ENCLOSED**	

CLIP AND MAIL TODAY!

139